THE LARRY & BARRY GUIDE TO
Entrepreneurial
Wisdom

THE LARRY & BARRY GUIDE TO
Entrepreneurial Wisdom

ARTHUR LIPPER III

SelectBooks

The Larry and Barry Guide to Entrepreneurial Wisdom
© 2002 by British Far East Holdings Ltd.
All rights reserved.

This edition published by SelectBooks, Inc.
For information address
SelectBooks, Inc., New York, New York.

First Edition

ISBN 1-59079-023-5

Library of Congress Cataloging-in-Publication Data
Lipper, Arthur
The Larry and Barry Guide to Entrepreneurial Wisdom–1st ed.

Manufactured in the United States of America

10 9 8 7 6 5 4 3 2 1

To Anni,
my wife and life of 40 years,
who continues to be so wonderfully understanding
and supportive, even in the face of some of the
dumb things I've done.

To our sons, Chris and Greg
and to their families,
of whom we are so very proud.

To those entrepreneurs and capital providers whose vision,
energy, courage and willingness to sacrifice creates
opportunity and wealth of many kinds for a broad range
of stakeholders, many of who are unaware of the
actions of their benefactors.

I say, "thank you for allowing me to be a part of your lives.
It has been a wonderful journey."

Arthur Lipper III

Contents

Introduction   ix

PART 1: Guide to Entrepreneurship   1

1 Getting started: The inspiration–source and   3
   validity
2 Sharing the vision–with whom, when and why   6
3 Describing the vision–how best to describe and   10
   why its best to play it down
4 The role you should play   12
5 Getting or providing money–cradle to pillow   16
   equity
6 Recruiting followers and other stage resources–   19
   without overplaying
7 Retaining attorneys   22
8 Goals and objectives   25
9 Advice for investors–the risks of being too early   29
10 First financing   31
11 More money needed–now what?   34
12 Attracting capital from family and friends–how   36
   to structure
13 What to do with the first non-personal money   39
   received
14 What's next–who can help make this vision into   40
   a business
15 How to attract capital from those you don't   42
   know...
16 Customer identification and seduction   44
17 Protecting intellectual property   46
18 Starting the business   48

19 Staffing   50
20 Banking   52
21 Insurance   54
22 Allies and enemies   56
23 Networking   57
24 Dealing with service providers   59
25 Dealing with partners   61
26 Running the business–Paying employees in stock   64
27 Planning cash   66
28 Product versus service   67
29 Maintaining the profit margin   68
30 Building accounts–understanding which accounts   70
    count
31 Maintaining cash flow   71
32 Selling the business–when and how   73
33 Selling the business–who can help   76
34 Selling the business–what and how to pay for help   79
35 After selling the business   81
36 What's next?   83
37 Valuing pre-cash flow companies   88
38 The making of effective presentations   93
39 Valuation approach re private company investment   97
    opportunities
40 Purpose and construction of business plans   106
41 Making an early stage, tough deal, possibly doable 109
42 Capital seekers reflecting their deal hopes in early 116
    presentations
43 Making investments appealing to professional   119
    investors
44 Fair question–for angels to ask entrepreneurs   134
45 The future of capital investing organizations   136
46 What I've learned from the mistake I've made in   140
    private companies

PART II: **Guide to Venture Funding**   153

Introduction

Lawrence (Larry) Lion and Bernard (Barry) Beaver are characters I created to personify the characteristics of many entrepreneurs. Larry, the extroverted, marketing maven, is always providing the energy and making the promises, whereas Barry, the inside partner, is burdened with the need to plan and deliver on Larry's promises. For many years, I used a Larry and Barry depiction to make a point in my monthly Chairman's Comment column in *Venture Magazine*—and, of course, I fell in love with the characters, as to me, they "said it all."

In many early stage companies one finds a partnership between an inside and outside partner, regardless of the legal form of entity. The fact is that starting and running a business requires both a lust for the future, which will always be perceived as being positive for the enterprise, by the Larry. Barry, on the other hand, is all too aware of the limitation of resources and a need for at least some of the good things Larry is counting on to actually occur. Of course, in some situations the Larry and Barry are combined in a single entrepreneur, who then must balance the need for optimism and for realism—which is no small feat.

Over the years, I have reached conclusions regarding many entrepreneurial endeavors and egocentrically deem these to be truths and therefore wisdom-like. These revelations have taken form in short writ-

ings and talk texts. This book is an attempt to provide a resting place for my experienced-based obser-
vations and recommendations. At the back of the
book there is reproduced the original *Larry and Barry
Guide to Venture Funding.*

It is my sincere hope that readers will find the
points made in this book useful in making decisions
regarding their own ventures. Of course, there are
differing opinions as relating to many of the points
made and as to individual situations. However, all I
can do is present views based upon my experience,
the breadth of which hopefully lends validity to the
views.

For those wishing to contact me, e-mail messages
to arthur@pobox.com is the best means of doing so.

Good luck and thanks for considering my perception of wisdom.

Arthur Lipper III

Part One
GUIDE TO ENTREPRENEURSHIP

Getting started:
The inspiration—source
and validity

Larry: *It can't miss. I don't know why I didn't think of it before. This is it, the Mother of All New Business Ideas. It's even better than the idea of charging $1.00 per call for predicting earthquakes over 4.0, by area code, for the next 3 days—and giving a money or even double money back guarantee if we were wrong.*

Barry: *Great. I can't wait to see the business plan you are going to get me to write. Is there a business model for this latest evidence of entrepreneurial genius or are we just assuming customers are waiting and willing to pay a price sufficient for us to project the level of profits necessary to attract capital?*

This is it. This is the solution. This is the idea I have been searching for. This is the business sure to succeed. Whatever "this" is, it's sure to be high potential and dangerous. The level of potential depends on how big a thinker the thinker is, and the danger arises from how strongly the thinker believes in and is able to sell the idea.

It is unfortunate but true that most human ideas and efforts fail to achieve the success envisioned by the ideas' creators.

Even ideas for the establishment of a new business comes from many sources. Something just clicks in the mind of the entrepreneur. There is a moment of revelation, almost an epiphany, when it becomes clear to the entrepreneur that a risk/reward ratio is heavily weighted in favor of reward—and it is likely the sophisticated capital provider will make sure the reward first comes to those financing the entrepreneur and then, after commercial viability is demonstrated, to the conceiver of the idea.

Sometimes the idea is conceived in a bed, in the shower, or at work or while doing something which is not all consuming of the creative individual's attention. When and where did you have your last really great idea? I'd wager it wasn't the result of sitting down in a quiet place after you decided to solve a problem. It just happened, right?

Now comes the hard part, separating the hope, wish and wants from the reality of the "what if's" list of things which can go wrong and therefore must be planned for.

All of us who are creative, and especially those who are serially creative, need a friend or loved one who can with care and integrity play Devil's

Advocate and poke holes in the fabric of our genius ideas. I am fortunate to have a wife (for going on 40 years) who had I listened to her experience-based and instinctive reactions and thoughts re many of my inspirations would eventually have been a far wealthier widow than is likely to be the case. However, if I had made fewer mistakes I would not have been as qualified to write this book or serve advisory clients as well as I am able to do. It's the mistakes from which one learns, not the successes.

Sharing the vision—with whom, when and why

Larry: *I can't wait to tell a whole bunch of people about the new business idea. They will line up to get a piece of the action and join our team.*

Barry: *Sure, and you really believe 1) they will all sign confidentiality and non-disclosure agreements and 2) these agreements really mean anything, even if we had the money necessary to sue people with whom we may again want to do business with and presently think of as being friends?*

Y ou have to tell someone about your new idea. Indeed, you'd like to tell everyone as it is so clear and logical and possibly important. One of the big differences between entrepreneurs and inventors is that inventors are innately secretive while entrepreneurs are incessantly talkative and sharing of their ideas. Inventors are concerned that their last good idea will indeed be their last good idea whereas entrepreneurs are all too eager to share not only the current inspiration but lots of other ideas they are not currently focusing on.

First, describe the idea for the business in writing. If the essence of the idea takes more than one type-written 8.5 x 11 page, using a size 12 font, to describe I suggest either the idea isn't so wonderful or you need help in creating the description. You must identify the USP (Unique Selling Proposition). What is the USP the idea will allow you to offer? Is it price? And if so is the price advantage at the sacrifice of profit margins? Is it utility? And if so can you distinguish the benefit from that currently in use? Does it make something easier for your customer? Is it a new way of doing something which is clearly better for your customer? What is the unique benefit being offered? Don't tell me how you are accomplishing your idea before you tell me why it is going to benefit the user.

Once you have a satisfactory one-page written description of the essence of the idea decide who, other than perhaps yourself, is necessary to make the idea a business. Do this by job function and not known individuals. However, before sharing the idea and deciding who you want to involve, decide on the relative (to your own) contributions the other person or people are capable of making and how badly (and when) you need them. I see and have been involved in lots of situations where people end up with a greater ownership in a business just because they happened to be there at the time of idea generation and not because they had unique contributions to make. I advise one company, which is immensely profitable, and which is still owned by the three founding partners, one of whom had the idea and primary ability to make it work and two of whom where his friends, one of whom originally provided less than $25,000 at the outset of the business. If the idea creator had reasoned through the process of starting up the business differently he would likely have retained more than a third interest in what has become one of our country's great marketing success stories.

Relatively early in the game you will want to share the idea description with an attorney as you will want to be in a position of engaging others in the pursuit of your dream, yet able to protect your own interests separately from those you've brought on board as well as others on whom you will become reliant.

Non-Disclosure Agreements (NDAs) are a necessary nuisance. Many of us refuse to sign them, at least until we are sure we want to become involved with the individuals and companies saying they "require" them to be executed, typically "on the advice of their counsel." Of course, in many cases the only reason the counsel advises the execution of an NDA is to provide evidence that a public offering of securities isn't being made by the promoter of the idea when in the process of seeking investments from ostensibly accredited investors.

The problem is that many of us who see a great many new ideas during the course of a normal week do not want to put ourselves in the position of unnecessarily incurring liability when two years from now, after having declined the opportunity of becoming involved with the presenter of an idea, we decide to become involved with another entrepreneur or group presenting a very similar idea that we find more attractive for some reason.

Although I am sure it has happened, I know of no instances where an entrepreneur's ideas have been stolen by professional investors or advisors. Conversely, I do know of lots of situations where entrepreneurs have been deprived of whatever assistance they might have derived from those who were unwilling to execute NDAs. In the end, the entrepreneur has to make a decision based upon the reputation of the people with whom he hopes to be dealing (and on his own instincts versus the "advice" of counsel, who usually has nothing to lose by offering some standard advice).

Describing the vision— how best to describe and why its best to play it down

Larry: *As you see we can only safely delay declaring profits until the 3rd year and then in the 4th and 5th years we are sure to have all the financial and operating leverage working for us. Our profit margins will be extraordinary and all of the securities underwriters will be clamoring to take us public.*

Barry: *Of course, to be conservative we used "worst case" numbers and then cut them in half as we only want to give our investors good surprises.*

"Describing the vision" is really describing the benefit of the vision to the identified customer base. As suggested previously, the initial description should not require more than one page. After the description of customer benefit, which is what your marketing plan will eventually be all about and which is the "why," you will want to describe "how" you will make the product or service.

As all with experience in this area know, everything seems to take longer and therefore require greater funding than has been planned for. Some of the reasons for delay, which is the enemy of the business owner, are legitimately beyond the control of the entrepreneur. However, many are a result of being overly optimistic or simply of underplanning.

The reader of the "making" part of the vision description will take the writing as being a promise of delivery and therefore the writer of the plan should adopt a very conservative approach to prediction. Indeed, as we will discuss later, many plans of finance will tie the predictions made by the entrepreneur to the deals being proposed and failure to achieve that which has been promised can result in significant penalties. The place to be expansive is in the vastness of the vision relating to the numbers of people to be benefited and not in describing how the product will be made.

The role you should play—what should be your role and how much of the business is the idea worth?...or...
Being an Idea Inventor rather than attempting to be a business manager.

Larry: *It's not that I want to be the CEO, it is just that I can't think of anyone better suited for the job. After all it's my idea and who better to make a business out of it?*

Barry: *Well some of the investors may think that experience in running a company successfully should be a requirement for the job of running our company. Also what makes you think that having been a frustrated middle level executive in a couple of companies qualifies you for the* *job of controlling the lives of the people we will be hiring and the money from the investors? After all, I am the one with the MBA—and it is just possible there are those out there even better qualified to run the company than I might be.*

OK, so you have had a great idea for a new business. How much is the idea alone worth as a percentage of the equity of a new business formed to exploit your idea? What role should you insist on playing in the new company? Is the business which may develop around the idea more or less important to you than the fun and power of running a company based upon your idea?

Most entrepreneurs present their ideas for new businesses with the assumption that they will be the CEOs, regardless of their experience or qualification for the role. I believe there are lots of good business ideas which never get financed due to the proposed management not being attractive to professional investors. Sometimes making money requires controlling one's ego more than most entrepreneurs are willing or able to do.

The entrepreneur having conceived the idea really should consider the pros and cons of participating in a successful business in which he or she has little or no involvement versus being fully involved and managing an activity mired in the need for fund raising.

It is conventional wisdom that professional investors prefer to invest in companies to be managed by CEOs having successful track records versus companies based on great concepts but managed by unknown entities.

The question of percentage original ownership is two part: one being a shared view of fairness, and the second having to do with leverage and idea protectability. As there is likely to be significant future dilution of equity interest as the business progresses, the Idea Inventor is better off having a revenue-based royalty than an equity interest, though of course both are possible. If the royalty interest results in substantial payments, then it is reasonable for the licensed company to want to exchange stock in the company for a termination of the royalty at some point in the future. Therefore the business proposition of the Idea Inventor might be one of "take my idea, and here are the reasons a well financed and competent management should succeed, in return for X% of the revenues in excess of Y$ [either cumulatively or per annum]." The terms of the arrangement can also include a reversion of the idea to the Idea Inventor in the event certain minimum levels of payment have not been made during an agreed upon period.

Although some ideas can be patented, the above proposal is not dependent upon a patent filing or issuance. Clearly, however, if the idea is patentable it would be better, in many but not all cases, to do so.

An idea for a business is probably worth about 25% of the original pre-initial funding equity of an early stage company. As subsequent financings will probably dilute the original investors by at least 50% and more likely by much more that brings the Idea Inventor's level of participation down to possibly as little as 10% to 12.5%. As the Idea Inventor is much better off with a percentage of revenues than of profits (which is the same as an equity interest) and assuming a 30% pre-tax profit margin, a royalty of about 3% of revenues seems about fair and probably generous for the Idea Inventor.

Getting or providing money from or by parents, close friends or even a spouse —cradle to pillow equity

Larry: *Sure, we can count on my parents and also on my two best friends to help us get started. The question is what to give them. They really are just trying to help us and wouldn't make such an investment for anyone else.*

Barry: *We have to give them a good deal, and probably should protect their capital ahead of the monies we've put in, including our credit card charges. The question is how to do it and still make a good deal for ourselves. Did you really promise them we would never ask them for more money?*

In my writings I advise parents not to invest in their children's companies. I do this on the assumption that it is not possible for the investing parent to negotiate a good deal in terms of shifting reward to themselves as the investor and risk to their offspring as the entrepreneur. The question is then: Why make any deal if you can't make a good deal? My advice has been—just give your child the amount of money you can afford to lose if the business fails.

In doing a bit more thinking about the matter I have now decided on an alternative course of action, one which is better conceived in terms of taxes. The new approach, and it works for friends as well, is to retain the would-be entrepreneur's company to do the research necessary to draft a really good report which could be also used as a business plan, one which defines the probability of success in realistic terms, so that the parents or friends can then make a better investment decision as to whether to invest— as can other investor prospects.

If done properly this should result in a deductible expense for the recipient of the report and ordinary income for the entity preparing the report. Subscriptions to investment-related publications and the purchase of other reports relating to investments are generally tax deductible. The entrepreneur can always, at a later date, reward anyone who has been of help to the company with stock or options. As with all tax-related issues the taxpayer is advised to check with his or her accountant or attorney before going this route.

Assuming the tax expert employed by the prospective investor agrees the expense of obtaining a report relating to an investment would be tax deductible, then it seems doing this would be more advantageous to the parent than giving the money as a gift. The recipient of the fee for producing the report would be the same entity starting the business and there would be sufficient expenses and losses for that entity to offset the fee income in terms of taxes.

Recruiting followers and other early stage resources— without overpaying

Larry: *Have you ever researched how much money the first 20 employees at Microsoft made? Do you know the personal sacrifices they made? Each of them have said they could have gotten jobs paying them much more than Bill did. They saw the vision and knew the fates had smiled and they were getting in on something really big.*

Barry: *We are presently researching the best employee benefit plans and deciding what will be in the best interest of those joining our team. As we will all be investing our lives in this business and want to keep as much equity as possible, we will be paying only minimum salaries. However, we will have great parties and be one large family, sort of like Microsoft, Dell and other winning companies.*

One of Arthur's Rules of Relationships that "in the moments of early stage attraction more is promised than is later felt to have been justified." Stated in coarser terms, many men would be better off if it were impossible for them to speak during or immediately after having an erection. Pillow promises have a way of becoming anchor-like.

I used to keep a sign on the wall of my Singapore office which stated "All loans appear sound at time of grant." Similarly, many early hires or personnel affiliations in new ventures seem to be more important to the success of the venture than proves to be true later in the development cycle.

All involved in a new venture should share and embrace the initial vision as to promise and necessity for delivery of benefits. All involved should understand the importance of their functions and contributions to the ultimate success of the enterprise. All involved should understand that a policy of the greatest good for the greatest number or enterprise benefit will be the only basis for making decisions affecting those in the company. It is not and will not become a matter of liking or not liking individuals whereas it will be the policy of the company to constantly evaluate the level of present value and potential for future value of each associate. "What have you done for me lately?" is a not an uncommon investor attitude and, in part, this will be reflected in the company's approach to valuation. Another sign one might hang in offices could read "Coasting Not Allowed—They Are Gaining On Us."

It is my observation that worker peers and subordinates frequently have a better understanding of who is really contributing to the overall good of the enterprise than do supervisors and senior managers. Therefore allocations of rewards such as stock options might most effectively be made based, at least in part, on the appraisals of those in the best position to observe the work being done.

For the record, I do not believe it is in the best interest of the company to pay attorneys or other professional advisors in stock or options to buy stock in the enterprise. There can be no doubt that owning stock or options in a company creates a bias for believing in a rosy picture of the future rather than being constructively skeptical regarding management's event projections as the"wish becomes the parent of the thought" so easily when success of the business has a wealth creation impact on the professional advisor. On the other hand, have less of a problem if the professional advisor is allowed to purchase stock for cash or even receive stock in part payment for a real and collectable note as the downside risk tends to bring about an objectivity options tend to obscure. Of course, the adoption of such a policy re the payment of professional advisors will result in higher cash fees being paid—and probably better advice and better quality advisors being available to the company.

Retaining attorneys (and consultants and other birds of prey)—some of whom really can and do help

Larry: *Look around at the trappings of this firm. They spend more on carpet cleaning than we will on staff training in the first year. I bet they also mark up the cost of the young associate who will be doing most of the work on our account by many times what our markup is on raw materials.*

Barry: *I've always been told the most profitable part of any law firm is the photocopying machine as clients pay a per page cost more than 10 times the cost to the firm. I also hear they make time charges to review and discuss their billings with clients. So, the more outrageous the bill, the more money they make in negotiating the amount they will accept in satisfaction of the original charge. Of course, they can't lose as they make the rules.*

Many professional relationships become unnecessarily unsatisfactory to clients because of the client's failing to properly define the role of and their expectations regarding the advisors.

Most of us feel our legal bills are too high. Most of us could, were we better organized and had a better understanding of the process, reduce the amount of time it takes lawyers to do their legal work of us. Although many lawyers will object to the thought that they are essentially drafters of documents instead of being advisors, the business owner is better off separating the functions of business advice from legal drafting. Of course, the more data the lawyer has and the clearer the client's instructions, the more efficient the lawyer can be, resulting in a lesser amount of time the client must pay for. I believe the client should do the first draft of what he or she wants as a document relating to a transaction; the attorney should then prepare the actual legal document, including in it all the issues and contingencies the client may have forgotten to include.

Clients generally do a lousy job of negotiating with their attorneys and then frequently complain about the size of the bill. The attorney is almost always more experienced than the client—and therefore in a position to take advantage of the client.

The best means of charging clients would probably be on a results-achieved, fixed basis. However, most attorneys charge on the basis of time (and, of course their client's ability to pay). This being the case, the client should ask for an estimate of the amount of time or money the complete delivery of a contract will require. As with any other form of contracting it is the changes from the original estimate that will kill the client in terms of additional charges over and above the estimate.

It is possible a fair arrangement could be one of the business owner estimating the annual cost of a full time general counsel capable of doing all the work the company needs and then negotiating with an independent counsel for a fraction of the amount of the full time counsel. If a General Counsel would cost, including fringe benefits, $125,000 a year, would the independent attorney accept $30,000 and agree to do all of the work necessary? And if not $30,000, what about $50,000?

Regarding independent counsel, clients have a right to know the amount and restrictions on the professional liability policy carried by their attorney. This policy may be an asset the entrepreneur may look to if the attorney does bad or dumb things.

My concern with using attorneys as business advisors is simply the fact that law is a precedent-driven discipline. All of legal training is looking backwards for comfort and verification of positions. Backward looking is not what is needed in advising companies re possible future events. It's the difference between planning and remembering. The business owner CEO has to look into the future and anticipate change whereas the attorney looks backward for reviewed judgments as to what conforms to laws and regulations.

Goals and objectives— why am I doing this?

Larry: *What do you mean what do we really want? We want to prove we can create a successful business. I want a corporate plan, lots of money for marketing, the power to hire the best people and to be number one in our field.*

Barry: *Fine, but who is going to be running the business 10 years from now and what will we be doing then? Also what percentage of the business will we own when it is finally a big success. Stop always talking about Bill Gates and think about all the other business founders who were forced out of the companies they started. I hear there is one venture capitalist who brags about having to replace the CEO in 72% of the companies in which he invested.*

Achieving goals and objectives is so much easier if said goals and objectives are defined.

What is the primary, most important, objective prompting you to take the risks associated with doing something new? Which of the following best describes your primary objective:

• Wealth—Creating significant wealth
• Income—Earning a large income
• Recognition—Achieving respect and acknowledgment as a person of worth
• Freedom—Weighing odds and taking action
• Satisfaction—Doing something useful
• Power—Making decisions and taking action
• Control—Having control over your destiny

Each of the possible primary objectives are natural desires for all of us but the exercise is for you to pick the one you want most to accomplish as a result of the idea you have for a business.

Once you have identified the primary motivation for going into business, you can start to think about how you will structure the business and the financing of the business so as to best be able to achieve your primary objective.

If you select wealth (the result of the company's value increasing—due in part to reinvesting income and *not* paying it out) try to retain as much equity as possible, paying your associates higher wages than you might were they to be equity holders. Give them high level bonuses and other incentives but retain the maximum amount of equity.

If income (what is paid out to the owner from the company) is your objective then arrange for you to be paid a percentage of revenues or profits for a long period of time. You can do this by licensing some critical part of the project to the company. Perhaps you should retain the ownership of certain elements of intellectual property or other assets and allow the company to use them for an ongoing fee.

If personal recognition is your goal, perhaps you can use your personal name in the company's name, as did Trump, Inc., Procter & Gamble and Hilton Hotels. You can also use your name in company-sponsored awards to customers, suppliers, the community, etc. such as the "James Blank Annual Award for Something."

If it's freedom you want, insist on retaining control of the Board of Directors and/or issue yourself shares having a disproportionate voting power.

If satisfaction is your primary objective, be sure you do that which is necessary to attract and retain the very best people you can identify and motivate. It's very satisfying to identify good people and then see them perform well. It's just like betting at horse races.

If power is what you want, define your job function as being the ultimate decision maker and be sure that most company decisions have to be, at least, approved by yourself.

If having control is of paramount importance to you, then, similar to those needing power, you are likely to be in a business where you have unique personal assets and are content for yours to be more a practice than a business. For example, an attorney can only have a practice as his ability to serve clients and charge fees is restricted to his life; whereas the owner of the building renting office space to the attorney has a business, as it can continue without the founder or principal.

Whatever it is that you want, a successful business can provide—as long as you plan and structure for it.

Advice for investors—the risks of being too early

Larry: *See, I told you it would work and that we should invest. Sure, it wasn't like inventing the wheel or fire but I knew there would be a good demand for the product.*

Barry: *You were sure right in recognizing the value of the product but it took 5 years longer than you thought it would and cost 4 times the amount estimated. We could have made the same amount of profit with less effort and sooner investing in one of the better performing mutual funds.*

D isappointment and unsatisfactory return on investment frequently result from knowing too much too early about innovation and new technologies.

Although it's wonderful to benefit from the information age in which we live, one of the downsides to being well informed about innovation and technology is the probability of disappointment if such awareness prompts early investment as there is such a lag between solution recognition and implementing production or inspiration and profit generation. The lag is caused by the need for risk taking financing and the natural resistance to change on the part of those threatened by change. Status quo is comfort and security to too many people in positions of being able to thwart or slow progress.

Investors should probably make relatively small bets in publicly traded and private companies as "place markers" to maintain an awareness of corporate and technological progress but not become disproportionately involved until later in the company's development cycle. Outstanding investment portfolio management success is a result of timely and disproportionate investment. Success in investing by professionals is measured not only by the difference between cost and market but more importantly by the comparative annualized compound return on investment achieved.

First financing—it's going to, and probably should, be you baby

Larry: *Well I'm in for all the cash I can get my hands on and can borrow from friends. I'm also going to max out my credit card to get this company started. We are going to become rich and although that isn't our primary motivation it will sure be nice not to have to ask anyone for money ever again.*

Barry: *I'll go along but I don't want to take on a lot of debt, so I guess I'll have to settle for a smaller piece of the action. Also, I'm a bit worried that all those bright and successful fat cats we talked to told us they didn't want to invest with us. Of course, they said "at this time." Does this mean we have to conclusively prove to them we don't need their money before they will deign to invest with us?*

The idea that entrepreneurial success is an exercise in using Other People's Money is dated and erroneous. Most successful entrepreneurs use a lot if not all of their own funds before seeking external assistance. They do this for several reasons. First, in the early stages of a venture only they are likely to see their vision clearly in all its potential worth. as it hasn't been clarified sufficiently, let alone found its way into a business plan.

Next, investment takes a range of forms. The entrepreneur in attempting to justify the size of promotional stock he/she wants in a venture will equate the time they have spent or invested in developing the idea for a business. They will assign a value to their time and then start multiplying hours and days and weeks, etc. This attempt at justifying a carried interest in the company isn't usually successful or appealing to an investor, nor is it necessary. Investors well understand that once successful the entrepreneur should profit from his idea and efforts. The other form of investment for which recognition is sought is usually expenses incurred in travel and entertainment doing the early stage stuff necessary to get a business started. However, as most who have "been there" will understand much of what is done in the earlier stages of getting a business started are wasteful as there are lots of blind alleys to be entered before finding the path through the maze.

The more fully developed the idea is the greater can be the valuation presented by an entrepreneur to an inventor.

My best advice to an entrepreneur starting a business with an idea is to keep a diary or log, both of expenses and contacts. Who was spoken to, where were they, what did they say, what were the expenses incurred in the meeting, etc.? Also, how and when plans changed.

More money needed— now what?

Larry: *I really thought we'd be further along by now. This isn't a good time to be going out for money. I can't put any more in myself.*

Barry: *I could put a little more money in but what should the valuation be? I should get a better deal than the next investors and at least the same basis as you got. Right? What's a fair valuation to ask our friends and family members to apply to their investment in our company? Of course, if it were not our company they wouldn't be willing to invest anything in the deal.*

One of the ever present balancing acts early stage business owners and promoters face is that until there are revenues or some other indicia of progress it is difficult to raise investment capital on terms the entrepreneur finds attractive. This issue can be addressed in two ways.

The first is to value the company very modestly and then have a series of ratchet notches where the interest of the entrepreneur is increased with achievement of specific events.

The second approach is for the business founder to sell a royalty on revenues instead of equity. Using this technique, the investor could be offered a high return on his investment, which could take the form of a loan, in the event the company was able to generate the revenues. In these transactions the entrepreneur has to be careful to structure the deal so that sufficient margin remains after the payment of the royalty as otherwise the company will not achieve profitability.

Attracting capital from family and friends— how to structure

The initial funding sources for most deals are the family and friends of the entrepreneurs, once the entrepreneurs have already invested as much of their own money as they feel is possible.

The problem facing an entrepreneur is how to structure and value the investment opportunity. I recommend in my other books that parents and friends do not "invest" in companies controlled by their offspring and friends, but rather effectively give or otherwise make available the funds they feel they can afford to lose, without buying stock or making a real loan. My theory is that as it is unlikely an investor having a close personal relationship with an entrepreneur can or wants to negotiate as good a deal as they would with an entrepreneur with whom they didn't have such a close relationship—why try to do something which is likely to bring discomfort either initially, or subsequently if the venture doesn't succeed? It's better not to have a "deal" than to enter into one less favorable than would otherwise be the case. It's not easy with a son to set forth terms on a take it or leave it basis. Also, it's not easy to enforce creditor rights when a close friend is the debtor. If the company is successful, the entrepreneur will always be able to recognize the contribution and if the company isn't successful what difference does it make as to how much stock one holds?

One approach to avoiding or, at least postponing the issue of valuing a company for a family and friends round of investment, especially the first such round, is to simply agree the money will be valued at say 50% of the next round of investment of over X amount, thereby, in theory, guaranteeing the initial family and friend round members a 50% notional profit.

The issue of valuation is difficult to disengage from that of managerial performance in meeting the objectives set forth in the business plan. What parent wants to remove a son from the presidency of a company which didn't meet its objectives and which used a projection of events that never materialized in attracting or justifying the capital infusion?

There is also the overriding issue of whether the company will become publicly traded or remain a privately owned enterprise. As a publicly traded company, the management and investors will probably want to report the highest possible level of earnings in order to attract investors and to gain and maintain a high price/earnings ratio. As a privately owned company, the natural instinct and motivation of management and owners is to manage the declaration of profits and to take a more conservative approach to reporting higher profits and therefore paying higher taxes. There are sufficient legitimate and legal options available to management for the two types of companies to reflect differing results for tax purposes. Therefore, in valuing a company while still privately owned the reality and timing of the company eventually having an Initial Public Offering must be assessed.

Most privately owned companies tend to be worth less than their revenues whereas mature, publicly traded companies which have increasing earnings tend to be worth a multiple of their revenues.

The minimum value increase resulting from the exercise of put options can be a reflection of annual percentage return on investment, as if the investment had been made as a convertible debenture or debt with warrants. Therefore the entrepreneur and the prospective investors can negotiate, perhaps more comfortably, minimum return of investment rather than overall company valuation and who owns what, though in the end it will come down to very similar needs to predict the future. For example, were the partners to agree that a 35% annual average compound return was satisfactory then tat return could become the basis for calculating the strike or exercise price of the put.

It should be remembered, the put is an option the holder has a right to exercise but is not required to do so. If the company is doing well then the holder of the put might be better served by simply continuing to hold the shares.

What to do with the first non-personal money received

The first thing to do with the first money received from someone other than yourself is to recognize that you have now become a fiduciary. You are now responsible to someone for the safety and enhancement of their capital.

Therefore, there is nothing, other than banking the money in a commercial bank account, that you should do with the money until you have collected enough money to achieve the objective described to the person making the money available to you. If the person providing the money is sophisticated about finances, there will probably be an escrow account mandated in which to hold the collected funds until an agreed minimum amount is collected. If there is no escrow account required by the capital provider, responsible entrepreneurs will nevertheless establish such an account on their own.

This is not to assume the objectives described to the capital provider will necessarily be achieved but it is to recognize that without adequate capital the objectives are most likely not going to be achieved. Escrow and other separate accounts expressly set up to allow the entrepreneur to accumulate adequate capital funds are one way of ensuring the moneys collected will be used in the best way possible for implementing the business plan objectives.

What's next— who can help make the vision into a business

Those having a combination of relevant business experience, a complementary vision to that of the entrepreneur, enthusiasm for the project and the people participating in it, absolute integrity and a desire to participate in the creation and nurturing of a business can help and should be identified and recruited.

The normal means of recruiting those having the ability to help is to grant them some form of participation, usually the right to purchase equity at what will appear to be bargain prices at some point in the future, when success has been, to some extent, achieved. Such rights have enriched many people and lured and seduced many more into becoming involved in startup businesses.

The greater the experience of the entrepreneur the more people the entrepreneur will be able to identify as being capable of making a contribution to the new enterprise. Investors should beware of the entrepreneur who is unable to identify those he'd most like to attract to his team.

Those having retired from businesses having a similar focus and characteristics to the one you're starting up make good candidates. Academics from both the sciences and from business schools can help a lot. Investment bankers and business consultants, both because of the range of businesses observed, can help.

How to attract capital from those you don't know and who have lots of alternative opportunities to invest, make and lose money

The art of intelligent, as opposed to wishful, investing is the organized comparison of alternatives. All of those having the ability to direct capital, regardless of the form of transfer of control, are constantly being presented with opportunities for capital enhancement.

Therefore, the entrepreneur seeking to gain control over the capital of others must convince those who presently control the capital that their best interest and that of those whom they may represent will be served by giving that control over to the entrepreneur in the hope and expectation that substantial profits will result. To succeed in that aim, the seeker of the funds is in a better position if he or she initiates the discussion of risk and defines the risk and then compares the risk being assumed with the profit opportunities being created.

It is my observation that those who have made the most amount of money on Wall Street are those who have paid the greatest amounts of fees and commissions. Financial intermediaries, and that is what brokers and underwriters are, are likely to be able to raise more money from investors than entrepreneurs on their own.

Of course, the financial intermediary needs the entrepreneur to play an active role in the luring of capital but it is the belief on the part of the capital provider or their agent, that the intermediary's presence represents an assurance of some level of due diligence investigation. Also there is an implied statement being made by the endorsement of the investment professional that on an alternative basis the investment is relatively attractive. Also there is an assumption on the part of the intermediary's customer that if it all doesn't workout as implied, if not promised, then the intermediary has the ability to make it right through inclusion in the next good deal—and so it goes. If you are an entrepreneur seeking funding, first entice the enticers.

Although it usually requires the energy, passion and charm of the entrepreneur to "close a prospect," the presence of a known financial intermediary represents a useful borrowed credability.

Customer identification and seduction—what is the unique benefit being offered?

Larry: *They are all going to be lined up to buy. We now have exactly what they need.*

Barry: *And by what divine guidance do we know this? Wouldn't it be better if we asked them what they wanted instead of presuming we know more than they do about their business?*

Rosser Reeves, an old friend and one of the legends of Madison Avenue, used to preach the need to identify the USP or Unique Selling

Proposition to his associates and clients. He was insightful.

Each customer of a business has needs and wants which are customer specific. The trick of getting a business order or a"yes" on a contract is to identify these needs and wants and to offer a matching product or service.

Wisdom follows—it is the customer who is in the best position of defining their needs and wants and the wise and successful vendor will simply resort to asking the customer time and time again, "What is it you want the most from the types of products and services we offer?"

Protecting intellectual property—and still being able to promote effectively

Larry: *What do you mean I shouldn't have told them the details of the benefit we can offer? It's going to save them millions and makes us almost as much.*

Barry: *I suppose you really believed the CEO when he said that stuff about their company policy of dealing with those who make a contribution—unless, of course, the CEO's brother has a big interest in one of our competitors or they can do it themselves without paying anyone.*

E nthusiasm is difficult to curb and we all want to talk and brag about that which we have which is new and different, especially to prospective customers. The more knowledgeable our customers, the more we naturally want to impress them with the genius of our product.

The problem is that in describing that which is not patented we may be creating a liability in that premature disclosures can be construed as "publishing"and as such cause a problem in the patenting process.

It is not only competitors which can use original ideas without paying for them; potential customers can also take unfair advantage of overly enthusiastic entrepreneurs.

Much as there should be a sanitized version of a business plan, one which does not disclose secrets, there should also be a sanitized marketing pitch. This is one of the areas where the advice of counsel should be sought as it is most difficult for those in the company to be able to really know what should not be revealed without necessary proprietary documentation protecting one's ideas having been executed.

Starting the business

Facilities—what's needed versus wanted

One of the realities of starting a business is that it will either be successful or not and therefore the physical facilities thought to be right will either be too much or too little as time progresses. Therefore leasing with the greatest flexibility is better than owning, and long term leases will probably have to be renegotiated.

Too many business startups are in reality only profitable to landlords and bankers (usually in the form of credit card companies)—assuming the entrepreneurs can meet their financial obligations.

Location—what are the decision points as to where to locate

Owner convenience, staff convenience, customer convenience, cheap rent, impressive appearance, flexibility in terms re use—all can be determinative of location selection and each, at a time in the company's development cycle, can be the clincher. Sometimes criteria can be very personal. It has been observed that when companies, usually publicly owned, move from Manhattan they tend to locate within a half hour of the CEO's country club or home.

How important will customer visits be? What are the staffing needs of the company and where will most of the workers come from? How expensive will it be to move to another location? Try looking ahead to the needs or the company 5 years out. Deciding on a location for a new business is never easy, and is probably one which is best made with the help of those familiar with local real estate (but with no commission involved).

Staffing—how to determine needs versus wants

Larry: *Of course we need him now. He knows all about the equipment we are going to make. Without him we'll never be able to make our schedule.*

Barry: *But with the comp package we'll need if we hire him, we won't be able to afford to market the product even if it does get made on time. Will he take stock options for half his salary? Can we use him as a consultant, advising us as we need him?*

When is the question, not **whether** about staffing. Many startup companies have, or want to have, people on staff significantly before they are needed, on a full time basis. They take the position that "we need the people because of their experience, and because without them we can't develop or offer the product." Perhaps so, but "when" is the issue and the entrepreneur must understand that time is the enemy since most projects take longer than planned for. Therefore any expenses not absolutely needed lessen the probability of success.

Banking—where and how

Commercial bankers, regardless of what they say, do not want to lend new businesses money. The banks which advertise proclaiming their interest in lending to young and promising businesses are being less than candid—as they will typically want personal guarantees of the primary shareholders and CEO. There is nothing wrong with their real position as they are fiduciaries and as such have to be primarily concerned with the specter of loss versus the siren of gain. What's wrong is their presenting themselves as something they are not—lenders to young companies versus lenders to those involved with young companies.

Companies should bank where it is advantageous for them to do so. What services can the bank provide other than loans? Is there a good chemistry with the individual banker? Will the banker make him or herself useful re business introductions and recommendations? Can the banks other offices be useful? Does the bank offer information resources the company can use? Will the bank cash employee checks? Does the bank do business with the company's customers and will the bank provide customer introductions? Will the bank allow one of its bankers to be on the company's advisory board?

Banking is a reference business. Who recommended the use of the bank? Was it the company's lawyer or accountant, who are both in positions to recommend a number of accounts to the bank? It is always better to be introduced and have it in the account record as a source of business to the bank.

Banks gain comfort from familiar letterheads. Bankers want the protection of a known party when being asked to establish a new relationship. Also bankers will treat an account differently and better if introduced by a party important, or a source of business to the bank.

Insurance—why bother and how to get good values

Writing and selling insurance is a competitive business because it is highly profitable to the insurance companies. The typical commission structure also makes it a relatively poor value for the insured, unless there is a need for the filing of claims. And, of course, once claims are filed then the other side of the insurance company's "house" comes into play and frequently denies or minimizes the insurer's liability.

To get the best value in insurance, shop the market. Use the Internet, contact several brokers and ask around. Do not rely on a college roommate or a friend who happens to be in the insurance business to get you the best rate.

In the end a well-advised investor will be most interested in the portfolio of insurance policies the company has purchased with the investor's money. There is also an issue of who should be named the beneficiary of an insurance policy. Should it be only the company or should those providing capital to the company also be co-insured?

Insurance agents are active in the business community and as such are in a position to be helpful to entrepreneurs in terms of contacts and introductions. Insurance agents can also introduce company executives to investment executives in the insurance companies they represent. As companies grow, the investment departments of the insurance companies may well be sources of future funding.

Allies and enemies—defining who can help or hurt your company

In every new business situation I try to identify and define who might be or become the natural allies and enemies. Who will the company help and hurt? How can those the company will help be of help to the company? How can the company protect itself from those who the company will likely hurt if successful?

Natural allies include employees, customers, suppliers, service providers and government departments and agencies. Make a list.

Natural enemies include present suppliers of similar products or services to prospective customers, other companies using the same sources of labor and other raw materials and government departments and agencies. Make a list.

What can be done to amplify the benefit to the natural allies? Can commissions be paid? Can intellectual property be shared? Can references be given?

What can be done to lessen the threat to the natural enemies? Can alliances be reached? Can agreements be reached which will neutralize some of the threats? How can the fears of the potential enemies be mitigated?

Networking—
why a necessary skill and
worthwhile activity

Once upon a time the "it's not what you know but who you know that counts" cliche was frequently valid. Less so today. Due to structural and communication changes in our society, there is an improved ability to identify and reach companies and people in a position to benefit from the products and services you are offering, even though you don't know, outright, the names of those companies or who works at them.

Although entrepreneurs are not usually "joiners" as they are typically non-conforming, membership in such organizations as the Young President's Organization (YPO), the Young Entrepreneurs Organization (YEO), the Chief Executives Organization (CEO), Gazelles.com, and even group therapy self-help organizations such as TEC, TAB, etc. can be useful. In most large cities there is a venture group and even though most of those attending meetings tend to be service providers there are useful contacts there to be made. In all cases, throughout this book, I assume the reader makes full use of the Internet, the world's most useful information transfer device. Most membership organizations have Websites and beware those which do not.

If you've identified a company you have a good idea for but with which you have no direct contact, you can still find a means of making contact with an executive of that company. If you are not able to do so directly as you are not known and there is a blockage in the form of a gatekeeper/secretary, your attorney, accountant of commercial banker may be successful. All you want is the attention of the executive for a very few moments so he can determine who on the senior level is most directly involved and concerned.

Dealing with service providers—consultants, professionals, advertising agencies, etc., for stock, promises and anything but cash

The rule is very simple. Those service providers who believe or want to believe in your business are or should be willing to "invest" their profit in your new business.

Therefore the issue is defining the profit of the service providers, and perhaps finding a means of promising something other than the immediate payment of cash in return for their providing immediate services.

Certainly in the case of most service providers such as accountants, attorneys and consultants, the service recipient can safely assume the cost of providing the service is less than half and probably only about a third of the billing amount. If this is the case, then, could it not be in both parties' best interests for warrants to purchase for nominal consideration the profit portion of the amount which could have been billed to be paid in warrants? In other words, why not pay the cost of providing the service in cash and allow the service provider to profit from the success of the business, on a riskless basis, through having an option to buy shares? There can even be an undertaking to register the warrants and underlying shares at such time as the company files a registration statement with the SEC.

Now, what do you do about the portion of the possible charges which represent out-of-pocket cost to the service provider? In most cases, these amounts will have to be paid in cash. However, it is certainly possible for hard costs to be paid in notes and/or percentages of revenues over an agreed amount, beginning as agreed and limited to an agreed amount.

If a service provider really wants to do business with a new account, there are any number of means of addressing the accounts needed to conserve cash for expenses which are not subject to accommodation. Cash is not the only medium of exchange.

Dealing with partners—how to attract, bond and when necessary separate

Larry: *Sure, we love each other now but will we, in twenty years, when we are both rich, still feel the same way? I won't forget how important both you and your wife have been to the success of the business.*

Barry: *Well, if we don't feel the same way, then we should split. You take my wife and I'll take the business—that way we both will have something valuable.*

Many successful business are started by partners, and when it works these relationships are a thing of beauty.

The partners bond, and their wives bond, and sometimes their children bond.

In many businesses, there is a need for an outside person, a "Larry," one who is the marketing-, people-oriented, high-energy extrovert. There is also a need for a practical "Barry" who worries about and manages the business from the inside. These partners comple-ment each other and do not compete. Together, they build and sustain the business enterprise.

Sometimes the partners were friends as children, sometimes they met in college, sometimes they worked together as co-employees. Sometimes they met in the course of a business deal. Whatever the genesis of the relationship, the two usually "clicked"and there was an instant recognition of their affinity for one another. Seldom do "Partner Wanted" ads produce real partnerships, and in most cases they are simply intended to find those having capital to invest.

Also, there can come a time in business relation-ships when partnerships must end. The need to end the relationship can be brought about by a change in the objectives or circumstances of the partners or a change in the nature and/or direction of the busi-ness. Sometimes it is simply a matter of a change in the health and/or non-business focus of one or both partners.

Whatever the cause, the termination of the part-nership can be, but does not have to be, destructive to the enterprise.

As with most issues involved in business and per-haps life, planning is the answer to a successful breakup. A "what happens if we no longer want to be partners?" discussion is appropriate before the busi-ness commences. Buy/sell agreements between the partners is a normal approach. In writing these agreements I try to avoid the artificiality of stipulating ratios and formulas but rather take the approach of the initiating party setting forth the terms of the proposed acquisition of the other party's (or parties') interest in the business. The recipient of the proposal then has an agreed time period in which he or she must either accept the proposal or purchase the initiating party's interest in the business on the same terms and conditions as proposed. Nothing fancy, just an assumption that those who know the business best will make as fair an offer as they can, knowing that they may, themselves, be required to sell on the basis they are proposing to buy. Incidentally, the proposal does not have to be all cash; it can include pay-outs, preferred or common shares (voting or otherwise), consulting agreements and a continuation of perks like cars and payment of other expenses, etc.

Reaching such an agreement is not as simple as I am presenting it, especially if the selling partner has relatives working for the company. Nevertheless, a reasonable solution can usually be found, frequently with the help of a third party.

Running the business—
Paying employees or
consultants in stock
or encouraging them
to buy shares

Larry: *I really believe all our people should be stockholders in the company. After all we are a team—and we can also pay them less in cash if we use stock as an inducement.*

Barry: *That's all well and good but as long as we are privately owned I don't want to have to make our financial statements available and certainly not to people who always want raises. Also, I see no advantage to the company to have to reveal more of our strategy and plans than we want to. After all, it's not as if our employees really invested anything for the shares—and why let them become a nuisance?*

It is reasonable for employees and those who assist in the creation of success of a company to share in that success, unless they have been adequately compensated on a current basis at the time of rendering service. However, the managers and primary shareholders of a company should avoid creating future problems for themselves.

I have seen a number of situations where employees and former employees were able to create problems for managers and majority owners of privately owned businesses which would not have been the case were they not shareholders.

Consideration can be given to the possibility of creating a profit-sharing trust which can be allocated by the trustee either discretionarily or based upon guidelines. Also, it is possible to issue non-voting shares to employees and others receiving the shares in return for service. The shares become voting shares only on a bona fide sale to an unaffiliated party. It is also possible for the employees and consultants to be required to place their shares in a voting trust for a period of time or until the company goes public or some other event.

In any case, there can be no more difficult or vexing shareholder, from management's perspective, than a former, dismissed and dissatisfied employee. Many of the problems are predictable, and can be avoided.

Planning cash—
don't run out of cash

Cash is only important to a business when you don't have it.

The constant playing of "what if" games is a key part of planning a business, and planning is a key part of running a business. The use of "what if" questions and spreadsheets are inseparable from the creation of survival scenarios. There are threatening "what ifs" to consider.

What if:
- the financing is delayed or not possible?
- the backlog of customer orders fall below X?
- the company losses one or more key executives?
- the technological development scheduled is late?
- there is a fire or other disruptive event?
- patent claims are disallowed?
- a competitor cuts its prices?

There are also good "what if" questions such as:

what has to be done if orders are greater than anticipated?
- what has to be done to enter new markets?
- what would be the result of raising prices?

Yes, the good "what ifs" are fewer than the threatening ones, but that is life. Greater planning is necessary for survival than for prosperity even though prosperity also has to be planned for and not just hoped for.

Product versus service— providing service while offering a product

All who are successfully in business understand they are in a service business even if the product being offered is a tangible product or widget.

The sale does not stop with the delivery, installation and/or consumption of the product. Customers either like or dislike dealing with anyone who sells a product or provides a service. Successful vendors keep asking the question, of customers and of themselves, "What more can I do to help and provide benefit?" We are all on probation for all of our lives and "What have you done for me lately?" is not always an unfair question.

Maintaining the profit margin —why do it if you can't make a profit

T he primary reason to be in business is to earn a profit. It is not the only reason to be in business, depending on one's personal definition of success, but it is certainly the most important reason.

The reality of business is that it costs money to produce a product or service. The pricing of that product or service is frequently beyond the control of the business manager. The market, including as it does the influence of competitors, may not allow even a company with great marketing skills to achieve pricing which will permit a profit on the sale of certain products. This being the case, when a company is unable to reduce its cost of production, the company must consciously decide if continuing to compete with that product is worthwhile.

To reach a valid decision, the company must gather and analyze data. Many companies really do not know their cost of producing many of the products they sell—and therefore are not able to decide intelligently whether they should continue or abandon the product.

One of the reasons I like to focus on investing in companies having intellectual property as a primary assets is that such barriers to entry allow for a better profit margin than in the case of companies having to compete on the basis of commodity product pricing. Companies with patent and other IP protection can price their products higher relative to their cost of production than companies selling products which can be readily copied.

Only companies planning for and achieving high profit margins are able to invest in research and development of new and improved products. The likelihood of profit margin maintenance is a crucial part of the investment decision-making process made by successful professional investors.

Building accounts—understanding which accounts count

The 80/20 rule does seem to work, certainly as applied to profits. Eighty percent of benefit does seem to come from 20% of those with whom business is being conducted. Of course, the exact percentages vary, but the premise that most of the benefit comes from a sub-set of the accounts being serviced is clearly valid for most companies.

Therefore, managers of businesses should identify and focus on the accounts from which the greatest profitability is expected—frequently relegating the less profit-producing accounts to lower levels of attention.

Serve well those who have the ability to be of great importance and give less attention to those who, even if highly satisfied, cannot become a significant customer. "Big fish eat little fist" and it's better to be of service to those who are big fish.

Managing cash flow—dealing with accounts payable versus negotiation of price versus stretching

All too often there is insufficient communication and collaboration between those responsible for negotiating the acquisition of services, for making sales and for managing the overall cash of a business.

To the extent possible, most business managers would like to operate using other people's money (OPM). The delaying of making payments to suppliers in one such approach. Companies such as American Airlines and General Electric are used as examples of companies practicing good cash management, albeit at the expense of their suppliers. I have no problem with such practices as long as those selling products and services to companies having a policy of delaying payments to vendors are aware of the policy so they can reflect that awareness in their pricing.

I have one very successful client company which does $100 million a year with its largest customer. My client needs account receivable financing but is reluctant to do as I have suggested, namely offer the customer an additional discount to pay more quickly than its normal 45 days. Therefore, my client ends up paying a finance company significantly greater interest charges than would be discounted from its customers' bills.

In general, I believe customers can be motivated to make payments more quickly, and I'd always rather enrich a customer than a finance company. Similarly, suppliers can be motivated to finance customers through the customer allowing for the charge of a higher than "cash in 30 days" price.

Selling the business— when and how

When to sell

The time to sell a business is when either it is no longer fun to run or there are buyers willing to pay more than the company is likely to be worth to the present owner in the next 5 years.

A business shouldn't be either a monument to someone or a means of providing employment for family members. A successful business is a living, vibrant organism which requires constant managerial attention and active leadership.

To have a feeling as to valuation of a business, one has to have an understanding of the valuation of comparable properties. The issue isn't so much what can be gotten for the business as it is what can be done with the proceeds of the sale once taxes are paid or provided for. In other words, what level of taxable or non-taxable income can be earned from investing the net proceeds of the sale? What other businesses might the newly liquid seller of the business now be able to acquire? How much of the proceeds will be available for new ventures? What will the health and energy level of the seller of a business permit in terms of new activities?

Most successful entrepreneurs do not create businesses with a view to selling them. Indeed, the decision to sell the "child" of the entrepreneurial parent is usually far more difficult to make than the decision to go into business in the first place. The process of going public is seen as a half-way house in that cash, a trading currency and personal recognition are created for the business founder (and those members of the team who may also have stock in the enterprise).

When to sell? Sell when there are other things you'd rather be doing than running the business and when others may be able to enhance the value of the property more than you can or wish to.

How to sell

Selling anything effectively is a matter of creating value for the buyer. In the selling of a business the objective is to demonstrate to the seller the provision of value and the benefits the buyer will enjoy as a result of the transaction.

The seller should act as if he or she believes the transaction will occur but also know there are many more negotiations and presentations than closings.

To understand the possible value of the business being offered, the seller should have a good understanding of the business as well as the needs and wants of the prospective buyer. Such an understanding will allow a prediction of the actions the new owner will likely take in terms of changing the staff and structure of the acquired business. In many deals, the seller's interest is for the buyer to have a good experience and to do well.

As with all interactions the seller should try to think as if he were the buyer prospect. What does he like about the business and what does he not like?

Does he trust the information he is being given, and if not, why not? Has he acquired similar properties in the past and if so what has been the pattern of due diligence and range of value considerations? Is the buying prospect's business on an upward or downward trend? What is likely to be the buyer's worst fears re the acquisition? Is he or she more concerned with overpaying, losing money, being embarrassed, missing an opportunity, etc?

If the seller's company meets its objectives and predicted results, is the buyer the most logical of prospects and will the value being sought then feel fair in retrospect after the sale? What can be done to assure the purchaser prospect of the company being a winner?

One approach might be to structure a transaction taking into consideration the Return On Investment made by the buyer re the whole company versus that applied to the seller's company. In other words, the seller could agree to either pay a rebate or extract an additional bounty depending on whether the ROI for the buyer turns out to be lower or higher than what was predicted.

Selling the business— who can help

Larry: *If they knew what we know about the new products they'd pay us twice what we are asking.*

Barry: *You mean if they believed what we know then they'd at least meet our offer. What we have to do is give them a deal where we are taking the risk of performance without allowing them to be in a position of being able to negatively influence that performance. Let's do a fair deal for the present package plus a royalty on sales over an agreed level for the next X years.*

Lots of people—most of them having their own agendas—can be of assistance to the owners of a business which is in the process of being sold.

Lawyers to do the drafting of documents, who may well have aspirations of being subsequently retained by the buyer and who will be able to bill more if the transaction is completed than if not. Accountants who similarly would like not to lose a client company. Advisors and intermediaries, some of whom may be expecting to receive a "success" fee based upon a completion of the transaction. Officers of the company, who will switch their allegiance on the closing to the new owner. Spouses and heirs who believe they will be advantaged by your exchange of operating assets for more liquid assets in terms of their own plans, some of which may have been disclosed to and discussed with the business owner. The bottom line is many of those most able to be of assistance look to their own future interests and such a focus may adversely impact the advice they provide.

Lawyers can also help by describing similar situations to the prospective seller of a business and warning as to pitfalls not obvious to those having less experience that themselves. Lawyers can make a critical difference, especially if they have had years of transactional experience. The selling of a business can be complicated and only a lawyer truly experienced in such transactions should be depended upon.

Accountants also have a wealth of experience in transaction involving the sale of a business and can, by the making of only a few suggestions, help the seller of a business end up with more net dollars as tax considerations loom large in most exit transactions.

Advisors and intermediaries do indeed typically have a "feel" of the market and do know, better than the seller, what the climate in the marketplace is and therefore can be valuable sources of input. An intermediary can also be used as a stalking horse, by indicating to the buyer a position the seller may want without committing the seller, in that the ultimate authority and ability to commit is usually left with the seller of the business and not his emissary.

The instincts of spouse can also be a good and sometimes final indicator of whether the deal should go forward. After all, the spouses know better than anyone the real needs and fears of the sellers—and share the frustrations as well as the anticipation of a relief from pressure.

The best strategy to apply is to identify those most critical to the process and make sure their objectives are aligned with those of the owners, to the extent possible. Advisors being compensated on a basis of receiving a percentage of the proceeds of a sale should earn a higher percentage with a higher price. Conversely, there shouldn't be a success fee or bonus paid if the price received by the seller is, agreed in advance, easily obtained.

At the end of the process there is usually only one decision maker on each side of a transaction, and they may even have bonded during the process as both want a successful conclusion to the deal. Also both know the best deals are those where both buyer and seller feel they have won—and can leave the bargaining table with a smile.

Selling the business—what and how to pay for help

Perhaps more than at any other time in a business owner's experience, advice is critical when involved in the process of selling a business. The personal chemistry between the seller and his or her advisors is important as the worthwhile advisor will frequently be in a position of having to tell the client exactly what the client does not want to hear. Therefore, it is important the seller of a business have genuine respect for the advisors he or she has selected. Respect is more important than a simple liking and trusting. The integrity of advisors as well as their knowledge has to be respected if adverse opinions are to be accepted and acted upon.

If the financial and psychological rewards to the advisor and the seller are aligned, the result will be better. The advisor has to have a passion to be of assistance and not view the transaction as just a piece of business. This is one of the reasons I believe advisors should be principals in their firms, not associates (let someone else pay the "tuition" for an associate's on-the-job learning experience). Perhaps even better, the advisor should be the senior principal or a proprietor of his or her own firm.

Of course, the seller should compensate the advisors whether the transaction concludes or not as otherwise the advisors could be all too tempted to press for a closing at any cost. Also, of course, the seller should be generous with the advisors if a completely satisfactory result is achieved.

If would be reasonable for the seller to agree in advance to a bonus pool to be distributed in the sole discretion of the seller, as a growing percentage of the proceeds of a sale. The higher the proceeds, the higher the percentage distributed to the bonus pool.

As to specific amount, it is impossible to make suggestions absent having details in hand. Nevertheless, a successful transaction should result in fees which earn the seller the lasting gratitude of the advisors.

After selling the business— how to remain involved and how NOT to remain involved

How involved do you want to be in a business you have sold? Is there any advantage to your remaining a consultant? Sellers are almost always going to become unhappy when they see how differently the new owners run "their" business. My suggestion is that sellers forgo the consultancy and instead wrap the economic benefits into the fabric of the deal. If the buyer really wants the advice of the seller, there can always be a short-term consultancy arranged.

If the seller of a business wants to remain involved in the field in some way, then perhaps the definition of "the business" might be expanded to include working as a consultant with trade associations or teaching some aspect of the business at a business school.

What not to do

What not to do? Staying on the board of directors is clearly one thing not to do. Another "not to do" is unpaid marketing for the company. However, a seller might consider becoming a marketing representative for the company or an independent agent for products similar to those of the company, as long as non-compete agreements do not prevent such a use of time, experience and relationships.

There is frequently a great temptation to stay involved. However, it is my experience that such involvement seldom is satisfying to the seller and can lead to unnecessary unpleasantness. One doesn't usually date a divorced spouse.

What's next?

Larry: *Before we sold the business and were still a good customer prospect he sure returned my calls fast enough.*

Barry: *There are two kinds of people in the world: those who take and return one's calls and those who don't. It's not so much the fact that we are not customer prospects that annoys me it's the contempt demonstrated by those who were so solicitous previously.*

The joys of teaching and advising—It's nice to be wanted and paid.

Thoughts for new stuff:

Larry: *This President wants to be remembered for supporting higher education. This means more government grants to universities, which should translate into more travel to far away places for academics. Academics like to travel and have been good at finding reasons why the Internet and other communications advances are still insufficient for their research.*

Barry: *Yup. We should start a business called "Successful Grant Application and Travel Agency" to help the academics. We also should be sure they get to keep their frequent flier points accrued as they wouldn't want their university or agency paying for the flight to get them as if they did the academics would then have to charge more for their time to get the same ROI.*

• • •

We are all on commission and only worth what we produce

Life is much like a row boat with lots of oarsmen. When one of the rowers stops rowing all of the others have to row a bit harder to make up for the loss of energy of the non-performing former rower.

Although function change and for some the universe of those they are able to positively impact becomes increasingly smaller, we are all still able to contribute something to someone—if we try.

Life is not about getting a free ride on the backs of others but rather is an exercise in collaborative labor —for both personal and community benefit.

• • •

Only that which can be measured can be improved

Improvement is a description of positive change.

Something is better, bigger, smaller, more useful, more productive, etc. In all cases there has to be a base case and periodic stages from which change is measured.

Therefore staff and personal measurement is necessary to know if a range of programs are being effective.

• • •

There is a natural correlation between staff and executive training and profits and p/e

It is natural that companies are measured by investors, competitors, customers and employees by the growth in competence and capability of staff. Such improvement is reflected in increased sales and profits.

Executive and staff education has a per employee cost. Companies making a greater investment in executive and staff education programs tend to perform better and sell for a higher price/earnings ratio than their competitors.

• • •

Test drive before buying—The necessity of probationary periods

One of the most challenging and necessary aspects of managing a business is that of identifying, attracting, recruiting and hiring good people. People, as with other assets, appear most attractive early in the process of familiarization. Whereas the sign I kept on the wall of the manager's office in Singapore read "All loans appear sound at the time of grant" the sign on the wall of a CEO or HR person might read "People are like bananas, after awhile the spots begin to appear."

It is really difficult to know if a key hire is going to workout or if they are going to like the environment and opportunity. Therefore, it can be a good policy to retain a prospective key hire as a consultant for a period of time before the final decision is made to hire them. For all employees a probationary period is a good idea.

• • •

Leaving money—They should be praying that you live rather than that you die

There are more important things to leave loved ones than just money. Money is, under certain circumstances, an appropriate means of benefitting heirs and satisfying personal emotional and psychological needs of the benefactor.

However, the gift of education and a value set which prizes independence and service to others is, in many cases, the best of inheritances. This, of course, assumes the heirs have the greatest gift of all, good health.

I have always believed parents fortunate enough to be able to afford it should willingly help their children in the establishment of businesses, with the full expectation of total loss of capital. The exercise of business creation, especially on a collaborative basis with one's children is a wholly positive experience and one which permits the parent to share more than money.

Also, why should loved ones have to wait until the demise of the parent for them to receive money—and therefore be conflicted and perhaps therefore guilt ridden at the funeral? Wealth transfer can occur before the benefactor's demise through a number of mechanisms including, gifts, loans, joint ventures etc.

Valuing pre-cash flow companies

Larry: *What do they mean our valuation has to produce for them an annual average return of at least 35%? We can't guarantee them a profit and we don't know what someone will pay them for our securities when they want to sell.*

Barry: *What they mean is that they want to buy in at such a low price that no matter what happens they have a shot at making a good profit. Two things. One, we have to be in business and need their money to get there. Two, we have a better chance of meeting our projections with their help than without it.*

In contemplation of offering expert witness testimony as to the appropriate magnitude of damages caused by a major company breaching a contract to provide service to an early stage business I have had to address the contention by the defendant that a company for which profits were not clearly predictable could not suffer damage as a result of the breach.

Even though such a premise is wholly theoretical and not of the real world there is a danger the exercise in sophistry might be found appealing to the unwary observer. The argument of the defendant is simply one of it being impossible to harm a company having a business plan, which the defendant claims, would never have been able to generate profits. Therefore, the specious argument goes "how could the actions of the defendant, or presumably any other entity, cause damage to the company which had to fail, even if everything had gone according to plan, as the plan was inherently flawed?"

Of course, such an argument is nonsense. It is much as a negligent surgeon basing his defense on the fact the patient would have died anyway, eventually and therefore the surgeon's actions were of no significance, except perhaps hastening the inevitable.

More importantly, those having to consider the fair and appropriate valuation of early stage companies must understand that in regard to both developing and marketing technology-based products companies many are started, not with a view to remaining independent until they mature and become profitable, but rather only to prove the efficacy of the product or demand for the product, after which they expect to be acquired.

It has become generally accepted that large companies do not start new enterprises. Instead, they use their much greater resources to acquire and exploit companies once they have demonstrated even only a modest market acceptance for their product or service. The large company justifies the payment of a premium price by their belief that they can improve on the performance of the smaller enterprise through superior management, economies of scale and bringing more assets to bear once there is an early indication of public acceptance of the product or service. Also the larger company has the important advantage of "brand" acceptance which can materially reduce the smaller company's cost of customer acquisition.

It is reasonable strategy for large companies to view themselves as opportunity portfolio managers and only to invest in the most appealing companies, those who have taken the entrepreneurial risk and shown the prospect of success.

A high percentage of currently successful companies were, at an earlier stage in their development, both cash flow deficient and non-profitable. It is misleading to suggest these companies were without value until they achieved profitability. Currently a large number of well known, publicly traded, companies are operating at a loss, either on the basis of the latest fiscal period or on an annualized basis using the latest reported quarterly results and it is equally silly to suggest these companies are worthless.

The value of a business is a function of its potential earning power and that is dependent on the resources, including managerial, which are available. The availability of necessary management and operating resources is, in turn, a function of the capital the business can attract.

Investors are willing to pay a premium for predictability and take comfort from planned progress being achieved. An unexpected event which disrupts the momentum and flow of progress can be sufficiently dislodging of confidence to make it difficult, if not impossible, for a company to regain its forward motion, thereby depriving the company's owners of the benefit of their investment.

In summation, early stage companies, as they have no history on which to base valuations, are dependent on the acceptance of predicted results as the primary basis for arriving at a valuation. The more closely affiliated the young enterprises are to established and prestigious companies the greater the investor confidence. Usually such collaborative relationships result in higher valuations and a greater availability of funding, as the existence of the affiliation is so positive in terms of investor acceptance of predicted events.

Perhaps most importantly, business plans are living documents and managers can and should change strategy and tactics as additional information is obtained as to the competitive terrain and customer response to early approaches.

If an arithmetic formula is needed for an overall company valuation, at a time of post finished product development but pre-cash flow generation, one times the realistically projected 3 year revenue level seems fair in many cases. This assumes revenues will commence immediately upon product introduction and not require government agency approvals such as would be the case with the FDA and FCC.

Young companies are the babies of business and are therefore fragile and dependent on the goodwill and acts of others. They seldom have all of the necessary resources of their own with which to accomplish their objectives Even with a paucity of hard assets having a value in liquidation they are frequently rich in potential based upon the vision, innovation and skills of those involved and all they need to fulfill their destiny is the slightest indication of success.

The making of effective presentations

Larry: *I make great presentations and do just fine with or without visuals. I'll wow them.*

Barry: *Sure you do, but tell them less about you and your vision for the company and more about the team who will be joining us and what our products will do for customers. You are not only applying for a job but also representing an opportunity. Lastly, don't make them think the whole deal depends on you. What happens if you get sick or worse?*

All of us present whenever we are with others and many of us present without the awareness of being "on stage."

Presenting effectively can be an exercise which is best accomplished by our not being our "natural" selves.

Effective presentation requires calculation and planning and has a clearly defined objective.

As with any other form of selling, the primary presentation planning objective is to understand and define that which the recipient of the presentation needs and wants.

Too many presentations focus on the presenter and the proposition he or she is representing. The objective of the presentation is not to demonstrate the ability of the presenter or the value and significance of the represented entity. The presenter who makes the data recipient feel diminished by the brilliance of the presenter loses.

Effective presentations are all about customer benefit, the customer being the recipient or audience for the data flow.

The following questions should be addressed:

Problem definition: Which of the customer's problems is being addressed and potentially solved? Is the problem specific to the customer or general? How critical is the problem? Who will be helped by the solution (what new equipment will have to be obtained and what new personnel will have to be acquired) and who will be hurt by the solution (what equipment will be replaced or personnel replaced or terminated)?

Solution definition: What is the solution to the defined problem? Why is the solution ultimately inevitable? Why is the solution logical? Why will the solution work? What will the solution cost? What will the solution save the customer? What added benefits, competitive and otherwise, does the solution bring to the customer?

Problem solver: Why are we in the best position to solve the problem and to receive the trust of the customer? Who are our people who are or will be responsible for the product or service delivery? What are our resources? What is our history of customer problem solving? When can we deliver and what will be necessary for us to do so? When can we start to solve the customer's problem(s)?

The above customer-focused points are in order of logic, not as is usually the case, in order of presenter ego or need to impress with the magnitude of accomplishment or power of delivery. It is the customer and his problem(s) which are the sole focus of the presentation.

In the case of presentations focused on attracting investment as opposed to the sale of product or services the following could be a adaptation of the above:

Investor's need: All investors have a need to identify situations in which there is a disproportionate balance of risk and reward, favoring reward. As the risk in investing in technology-based companies is total the rewards have to be sufficiently impressive to justify the financial and decision maker's career risk exposure. Those having the fiduciary responsibility of investing the funds of others also have a personal and organizational need to gain early access to information as to that which is likely to disrupt the businesses in which they are involved or which have been under consideration. The investment manager has to determine if the opportunity presented is akin to that offered early stage investors in a range of winning companies and strategies. There is a significant risk to not investing once the presented data is understood and verified.

Solution definition: Winning in investing is having created wealth through the application of knowledge and conviction-based courage. We are supplying the basis for knowledge transfer. An investment in our company can possibly result in a total loss. However, we believe, for the following reasons, that a gain of major proportion is the more likely outcome.

Problem solver: We offer as indication of our ability to complete the task the following technology and intellectual property assets. More importantly the following people, each having a recognized knowledge of the area, have invested their resources and reputations by investment and affiliation. The terms of the proposition being offered are such that if we are successful the magnitude of the gain will far offset the possibility of loss.

I hope the above is useful to you, as you are my customer.

Valuation approach
re private company
investment opportunities

Larry: *They fell for it. That was a great idea of valuing the company at the same average price/earning ratio as Texas Instrument, IBM and Microsoft five years from now. Let's say the average p/e is then 20 and we make our projections...we'll be billionaires.*

Barry: *Sure it sounds fair but if we only make a quarter of our projections or don't have any earnings then the deal isn't so wonderful. And note they suggested using mature companies, which won't have the same high p/e's as companies that have grown their earnings as fast as we will have.*

"How much do I get for what I give?" is the basic question asked by an investor considering an investment in a private company. Of course, some of us believe the question should also include "and what is the probability of my getting my money back and when?" It is the "when" which is used to determine the competitively all important Return On Investment (ROI).

There are lots of venture capital industry utilized approaches to the valuation of companies and therefore the securities they issue, and many are quite academic and too theoretical for my taste. The valuation of a company, based upon a review of the past and an appraisal of the future, is usually the basis for the terms of a transaction as proposed by a professional investor. All valuations require the generation and at least partial acceptance of projections of revenues and earnings, within a specific period of time. Most professional investors will discount, at least, the revenue timing projections of the entrepreneurial manager and therefore probably will have a lessened proposed valuation than would be the case were the projections to have been fully accepted.

I believe the process is or should be one of the initial focuses of the investor making a decision as to whether he wants to be an owner of the business, present or prospective—at any price or valuation. Does he want to be in that particular business and does he want to be in that business with the specific people as managers? Only after an affirmative answer should the issue be the valuation of the enterprise, as implied by the terms sought by the entrepreneur or seller of the securities.

A significant part of the normal valuation process is the price based ratios of publicly traded stocks issued by companies believed to be comparable to the privately owned company in which an investment is being considered. Of course, no two companies, especially when one is privately owned and the other publicly traded, are fully comparable. It should always be recognized that public company market valuations are made by the last sale, irrespective of either volume or supply of shares which might be available or wanted at that level. If a lot of stock cannot be either bought on the offer or sold on the bid how realistic is it to use a last sale price as the multiplier of outstanding shares to calculate market value?

Issues relating to the publicly traded company such as the history of the companies, the timing of the public offering, the quality and substance of the companies' sponsorship, the quality and ferocity of the public and investor relations effort, the strength and dedication of the company's supporters, brokers and market makers, the amount of shares trading in the float as a percentage of the shares outstanding, the record of the company in achieving projected results, the number of alternative stocks in similar businesses which are trading, the market's appraisal of management, the actions of management re buying or selling shares of the companies, the trend of the general market as well as the specific industry segment and the trending of relative (to market and industry measures) of such factors as sales per employee, change in the sales per employee versus a prior period (which is one of my favorite measures of management strategy and efficiency), balance sheet ratios, revenues and revenue changes, earnings and earnings (or losses) change, are all part of the landscape which must be studied. It is not easy to make direct comparisons, though we all try.

Before going further, I wish to review some truths and opinions. We all want to make as much on any investment as possible while exposing our capital to as little risk as possible. We also want to make as much money as possible in the shortest amount of time possible. As the venture capital investor is so dependent on the level and trend of the stock market there are clear, though unfortunately usually only in retrospect, windows of opportunity. It is in these windows that actions have to be taken to maximize profits and minimize losses. Markets do not wait for investors to use them or announce when changes are going to occur. They happen and the successful investor is prepared to use the markets for his advantage. For example, in the case of a company wishing to access public markets, has the paperwork for the IPO been done, have the necessary approvals from the Board and shareholders been approved and has the underwriter been identified and pre-negotiated with?

In recent years, the greatest cause of losses incurred by American professional venture capital investors has been their trying to invest too much money too quickly. As a result, currently, I believe there is a significant personal liability on the part of the General Partner managers of American venture capital investment partnerships which are in a loss position. The possibility of such a personal liability has never been previously taken seriously.

Regarding risk exposure—what about purchasing risk insurance in some form? Risk reduction can take many forms. The most common form currently being applied in difficult to finance publicly traded companies is the so-called "death spiral convertible"or "toxic preferred." In these cases the capital provider either makes a loan or buys a preferred stock with a conversion feature which allows the purchase of shares at stipulated discounts to the market price of the shares being traded. Therefore, the lower the price of the shares the more shares can be bought for the same amount of money, thus reducing the risk (or increasing the profit) on the transaction. In most cases, companies forced to accept funds using these instruments do not survive. There is an ever present suspicion that the capital providers have taken short positions in the shares so they benefit from the decline in the price of the shares as well as having the ability to profit in the unlikely instance of the shares increasing in value. It is not a pretty business but desperate people do desperate things—and mostly live to regret it. Some of us hope there will be some form of regulation enacted limiting such abuses as investor losses cannot be in the public interest. After all, there are usury laws which are intended to protect borrowers and corporations desperate for stay alive capital also need protection.

The toxic preferred is an extreme variation on the more normal ratchet provision of a venture capital financing where the conversion ratio of the preferred share is determined or adjusted by the earnings (or revenue) performance of the recipient of the capital as relating to projected levels made in the original seduction of the capital.

I have always believed there can or should be insurers for all or a part of the capital risk in private company investing. It should be possible for a capital provider to obtain a third party indemnification for a portion of a loss. In the early 1970's I started a company in Singapore, First Loss Guarantee Corporation, through which we offered business owners an instrument with which they could obtain better terms from banks or even bank loans when without the first loss guarantee no loan would have been available. In this case, we were willing to take the first loss. Why not an indemnifier willing to take the bottom tranche loss for a fee and/or part of the upside?

My approach to financing private companies is a bit different. I start with the premise that the company receiving the funds has to recognize that I have a minimum return on investment (the amount of capital exposed to risk) and the terms of the deal will have to produce a result which is satisfactory. To the extent possible, we want to focus on and lessen risk versus attempting to maximize return. Our target ROI is to earn 3 times our capital in 3 years or a 44% annual average compound return. And it would be fair for you to inquire if we achieve our objective— and the answer is sometimes but not on an overall basis.

As a rule, we prefer to guarantee bank loans rather than purchase equity. We prefer the guarantee approach to that of making direct loans, even though we provide the bank with 100% collateral coverage on the guarantee, usually in the form of Letters of Credit though at times securities are used. It is our experience that it is better for us to be a guarantor than a lender as the bank is more likely to be important to the borrower than we are. Also it is good for the company for the bank, as selected by the borrower (and approved by ourselves) to become familiar with the company as at the end of the loan period, usually one or two years, the bank may be willing to provide an unendorsed credit or one which is less than fully guaranteed.

Now why would we expose capital to risk in endorsing a loan for a company with a bank of their selection? We would do so to help the company and to earn a guarantee fee. The form of guarantee fee can be a fixed amount plus an additional consideration ranging from cash to equity or warrants to purchase equity. The fee can also be, as we prefer, a royalty or as we describe them, Revenue Participation Certificates (RPC).

The RPC or royalty can be for a:
- fixed percentage of sales, say 5%,
- fixed percentage of sales over a minimum amount, say $2.0 million,
- fixed percentage of sales up to a maximum with a declining percent thereafter up to other levels,
- varying percentage based upon revenue, increasing or decreasing with increasing revenues,
- capped or maximum amount per specific period and/or
- minimum amount per specific period.

The RPC can be:
- secured by a pledge of all or specific assets,
- guaranteed by a third party as to either or both principal and interest of the loan or fee payments due to the guarantor,
- convertible into equity and negotiable and distributed at the discretion of the guarantor.

As will be noted, there is a wide range of opportunity for creative financing in the use of RPC's. However, we have not yet addressed the most important issue regarding royalties or RPC. The most important part is maturity. For how long is the beneficiary of the guarantee responsible for making payments to the guarantor?

The recipient of the guarantee usually believes the RPC payments should terminate at the time the risk is eliminated by the loan being repaid and the guarantor released. I, on the other hand, believe the payments should continue for a much longer time, possibly in perpetuity.

When I originally guaranteed a loan for the then publisher and founder of *Venture Magazine* for $3.0 million with which to purchase and finance the magazine the deal was for a guarantee fee of 3% of annual, not cumulative, revenues up to $5.0 million and 5% on all revenues in excess thereof—for 35 years. When the publisher asked me why 35 years I told him because I thought 36 years too long. Incidentally, the deal was a disaster for me as when the loan wasn't repaid and the company couldn't go public as the publisher had planned, I ended up taking over the management of the publication, which I had come to love, and continue to pump money into the beast. I made most of the management mistakes I lecture and warn people about and it ultimately cost me many times the amount of the original loan. However, in many ways it wes also my best investment even though financially it was a dramatic loser.

In any case, the recipient of the guarantee and party obliged to make the guarantee fee payments, which incidentally can be daily, monthly or whenever revenues are received as there are no profit and loss calculations involved, should, in all fairness, have an ability to make a payment to terminate the on-going obligation. Such a termination payment can be adjusted as to the time of receipt and also relate to the monies already paid.

As with most providers of venture capital, we think in terms of how many times we replicate our money as exposed to risk and in what period of time. A five times return is great in two years (124% annual average compound return) but is only a 38% annual average compound in 5 years. The problem with a 38% compound return is that it is insufficient to make up for a lot of losses and losses are inevitable in venture investing, no matter how sophisticated the capital provider.

Purpose and construction of business plans

Larry: *They will be really impressed with our projections and how quickly we can deliver profits for so little money, relative to their funds.*

Barry: *Face it. Our projections are a big loss first year, a smaller loss second year, break even third year, a small profit fourth year and a big profit fifth year. Just the same as all the other business plans. Wouldn't it be better if we asked them how they wanted their money invested by us and how fast they wanted us to move?*

There are several purposes in preparing business plans.

For many, the primary purpose is to obtain an audience with a prospective capital provider, who will usually require a prior submission of a business plan before agreeing to a meeting. For others, the reason to do a business plan is to study and justify the allocation and expenditure of resources, perhaps available from within the larger enterprise.

I have recently, in a discussion with a corporate consulting client, reached the conclusion that business plans can be developed differently and more constructively than is usually the case on the traditional business plan. Incidentally, almost all plans have the same "hockey stick" presentation of financial projections. This annual "down a lot, down a little, break-even, up a little and up a lot" prediction series is more likely to be accurate in the early years than the later years.

The first part of the business plan, or business description, can be simply a non-predictive description of the business as it physically exists now.

The second part of the business plan can be a three part presentation of possible courses of action. Each course of action would have a different, objective, required investment and risk/reward profile.

The first objective might be maximum possible growth of revenues and/or profits, in the shortest amount of time, using the minimum amount of resources. Certainly, allowing a greater amount of time and employing more funds are options which will also be explored.

The second objective might be maximum assured growth of revenues and/or profits. In this case the time required and level of resource application will be more precisely known than in the "maximized" case.

The third objective might be a favorable balanced risk/reward result where the level of resource application will be somewhere between the first and second cases.

The singular advantage of such a breakdown in a range of corporate objectives is one of the independently investing capital provider, or a board of directors, then being in a position of being able to select how the selected management is going to spend the provided capital. In such a program the capital provider could elect to participate in the development of the business as it best suited the investor's needs.

The reading of a business plan should improve the reader's understanding of the current business and the prospects for the business, if operated under one of the described optional programs. The problem posed by conventional business plans is they present the management's (or business plan author's) conclusion without providing a way for those who are expected to pay for the process to exercise their own judgment as to possible alternatives.

I believe it is the board of directors of a company which has the responsibility of establishing the course of action management should follow and not be put in the position of simply authorizing management to proceed as they propose, without a full exploration of the alternatives.

It all comes down to a definition of success which is agreed to by all of the significant parties to a transaction. Once the definition of success is accepted then the alternative courses of action can be more effectively analyzed and the defined success more likely to be achieved.

Making an early stage, tough deal, possibly doable

Larry: *Their deal stinks. If we fail to reach our minimum projections they end up with so much of the company they control it. Also, in the meantime they own all of our assets.*

Barry: *Right but remember these are our projections, not theirs. We could always make them even more reasonable. Also if we can't do the minimum what they will control is a company which either has to be closed or will need lots more money. And if we do make our projections we get pretty much what we wanted in the first place.*

In my on-going attempt to help both entrepreneurs, seeking difficult to obtain capital with which to pursue their vision, and investing capital providers, who if they lose their money in one of their early private company investments are less likely to fund other projects, I propose the following structure for consideration. The basis premise is one of the investor being optimally protected and advantaged in the case of projected events not occurring as predicted.

1. **Re market segment and vision**—The capital provider must have good reason to believe there is a need for the company's product and the market segment is large enough to make an investment in the company attractive to those having confidence in the technology and validity of the intellectual property. This assumes the investor is comfortable with the anticipated competitive position of the company and has confidence in the management of the company and its ability to raise and subsequently manage the necessary capital.

2. **Re CEO**—The capital provider must find the CEO and other senior members of the management team honest, intelligent and articulate. They must be able to present well and communicate their vision. The CEO must be forceful and have an acceptable level of business sophistication to be the person responsible for the company's negotiations.

3. **Re staff**—The capital provider must have confidence in the senior staff and not just the CEO. Investing in an enterprise based upon respect for and confidence only in the CEO is investing in a practice, not a business. Practices, such as consulting, medical, legal and other professional firms, even successful ones, tend to have a market value of one times revenues. Successful businesses tend to sell for a higher valuation and the cap-

ital provider should be confident that others than just the CEO can achieve the predicted results.

4. **Re capital structure**—Companies reach a point of having to raise capital quickly and therefore must create and present a capital structure which is appealing to prospective capital providers. If the company cannot be financed then all monies previously invested will be lost. The structure should be based upon a combination of the prospects for the company and an awareness of the current general market conditions for capital raising for similar ventures. The reality is that previous investors, in situations where the company will cease operation or not be able to start operation, without the receipt of additional capital, have already lost their money and therefore their cost basis and the market capitalization implied is of no consequence to the prospective capital provider.

5. Possible terms to make an offering competitively attractive might be:

   A. **Form**—Senior, secured, minimum guaranteed return, convertible debenture

   The investor should want the company's obligation to repay his loan before all others if the funds provided are sufficient for the company to reach a position of being cash flow positive.

   The investor should want, to the extent possible, to have all assets of the company pledged or be subject to a Uniform Commercial Code (UCC) lien favoring the investor if the company is unable to meet its obligations to the investor.

The investor should want to believe the funds provided to the company will receive at least an agreed Return On Investment, perhaps the same or more than would have been the case if investing in an S&P 500 index fund.

The investor should want all of the protection of a debt holder until such time as it is in his best interest to convert into equity. It is the conversion feature of the debt instrument which provides most of the upside rationale for the investor accepting the risk inherent in the transaction.

B. **Maturity**—36 months

Although 36 months is not usually sufficient time for a company to be able to repay a loan from its cash flow it is, depending on the company's projections, usually sufficient time for the company to arrange a refinancing of the debt by selling equity or other securities on more advantageous terms than is possible presently—if the projections have materialized.

C. **Amount**—as necessary to achieve positive cash flow

Entrepreneurs and managers must realize that time is their enemy and that almost always they underestimate the time necessary to achieve their goals. Therefore they will need more operating capital than projected. Therefore, they should get enough money to reach a point of being cash flow positive. Running out of cash is not a place to be as it tends to disrupt a lot of plans and dreams.

D. **Interest**—Relative versus absolute

The investor in a private company deserves and should require a premium interest rate to that available from a broad market index. The amount of premium is subject to negotiation, especially if the investor agrees to wait until maturity to receive the interest. Therefore, a 50% premium seems reasonable. LIBOR, the London Interbank Offered Rate, is a measure of interest rates for international loans which appear to professional investors as being relatively riskless. Therefore, 150% of LIBOR, paid at maturity should be attractive, even if the company has the right to pay the interest in its own shares, if the company's shares are then publicly tradable.

E. **Conversion**—as negotiated but with a ratchet based upon management's prediction of revenues and other events such as the allowance of patent claims

All investors in private company subject their capital to risk based upon an anticipated return and that anticipation is based upon management predicted events. Therefore, if the predictions turn out to have been unduly optimistic the investor has taken a greater risk than had been contemplated. The protective device most often used by professional investors to guard against becoming the victim of entrepreneurial enthusiasm is the ratchet. In its simplest form the investor's stake in the company increases, without additional investment, by an agreed amount in the event predicted events do not occur.

F. **Guaranteed minimum return on investment**—of say 125% of the return of the S&P500 (on a dividend reinvest basis) in the form of a "put" (an option to repurchase the debentures, at maturity, at the option of the investor).

Much as the interest payment obligation of a company can be relative to a market measure so can be the repayment of principal. If the general stock market increases by X% in the period of time the investor has denied himself the use of capital which might have been invested in an index fund, shouldn't the investor be assured the value of his investment in the private company will increase by at least as much? The justification for the premium is that of the lack of guarantee the company will be able to meet its obligations and the capital provider may lose some, most or all of the capital exposed.

G. **Collateral**—the present and future intellectual property of the company.

Most early stage companies have little, if any, assets which can be used as collateral for loans, except for their intellectual property. Indeed, the value of the intellectual property is frequently difficult, if not impossible, to accurately assess. Therefore the capital provider might consider purchasing, for nominal consideration, all of the company's intellectual property, licensing it back to the company on a royalty free, exclusive, worldwide, basis and giving the company an option to buy the intellectual property for the same

nominal consideration as the investor paid—
at such time as the company met its other
obligations to the capital provider or the
investor converted into equity.

The above is an attractive investment for an
investor believing the company has competitively
attractive technology and intellectual property and a
business plan which can be executed by the identified management all of which will allow the company to become cash flow positive and meet its obligations at the end of 36 months.

The fact that most human endeavors fail to
achieve their objectives does not mean entrepreneurial pursuits should be curtailed or abandoned. It
does, however, mean that those who wish to stay in
the game of vision financing should protect, to the
extent possible, the capital for which they are
responsible so that it can bring benefit to ever
increasing numbers of people.

Capital seekers reflecting their deal hopes in early presentations

Larry: *Of course, we should tell them up front what we want. If you don't ask you won't get. Besides we have to get them thinking about the true competitive value we and our products represent. We also have to let them know how sophisticated we are in deal making. All we need from them is a "yes."*

Barry: *Sure and they have never made a deal before and are really going to be influenced by our first proposal. The only thing we will accomplish by presenting our hoped for deal is to have them decide not to bother reading our plan. Our job is first to get them interested in us—at any price. Also we can always say "no" to their proposal—if we are so lucky as to get one.*

Does anyone believe those seeking mates should wear t-shirts or have posters made displaying their "required terms for bedding and mating?"

The sole function of presenting a business plan or other introductory document to a prospective capital provider is to create an interest in participation and involvement.

Why, therefore, present that which may constitute an initial impediment or factor which distracts the prospect, who will usually simply discount the entrepreneur's valuation as being irrelevant to their primary focus of deciding if an involvement at any price is desired.

Of course, when meeting with either new investment banking clients or those seeking capital from me as an investor, I ask the entrepreneurs for their ideas of valuation. I do this to simply to ascertain if they are in my "real world" of valuation, as if not I'd rather pass on the project completely rather than waste their or my time and emotion.

If an agreement can be achieved as to likely earning levels based upon assumed future revenue levels then structuring a deal which meets the needs of all concerned is easy. Therefore the entire focus of the introductory exercise should be the creation and presentation of a sound and logical case for the projection of future profit levels.

One does not even have to precisely define future price earnings or revenue ratios as it is possible to use those same ratios for identified stocks or an index of stocks as being the basis of a deal. In other words, the investor's interest could be X% of the company's stock at a valuation of 50%, 100%, 150% or X% of the price/earnings ratio of the agreed valuation measure in an agreed year (of course, subject to fair play and standard accounting practice).

As a capital provider I am interested in what the capital seeker can do for me in terms of capital enhancement of the funds for which I am responsible and not what I am expected to do for the capital seeker in terms of his or her enrichment. I want them to be enriched as a result of their making my capital grow and that is what they have to show me will happen for me to be interested in their project.

Making investments appealing to professional investors

The plight of the entrepreneur is usually one of not having available sufficient capital to manage the challenge of starting or growing a business. Most businesses are initially financed by the entrepreneur, using the entrepreneur's own capital and that which he or she can borrow. The next step in the process is that of inviting the participation of family and friends, those who presumably are more interested in helping the entrepreneur than they are in creating the most favorable investment possible. In other words, they are more heart-based than brain-based investors. Of course, in some theatrical project investments still another capital provider organ influences many transactions.

This is all fine and the way most, in numerical terms, businesses are financed as professional investors, including the so-called venture capitalists, have no appetite for the vast majority of businesses. Their lack of interest is based upon the focus of the business, the scope of the business, the relatively modest amount of funds which can be effectively employed in the business and most importantly their assessment of the quality of management of the business.

Therefore, many entrepreneurs are left with the task of creating business opportunities which are and can be presented to professional investors in such a manner as to appeal to them and possibly resulting in the business being financed.

When I start to read a business plan, and it is important to recognize that even I, a lone practitioner who makes no attempt to solicit the submission of plans, receives several a week from friends of friends and acquaintances of acquaintances and also from those who approach me without the benefit of an introduction, I have a process of reviewing plans which may be of interest to you. I first read the first few paragraphs of the Executive Summary and then go to the management section to see who is going to manage the money the company seeks. I am always surprised by the number of plans I read where at the end of a few pages of the Executive Summary I have less than a clear idea of what the company does or wants to do.

Entrepreneurs should tell me, as a prospective investor, right up front, who the customers are or are expected to be for the product or services the company offers or hopes to offer. Tell me why the company has an advantage over larger, better financed and more credible competitors. Tell me why the company is going to survive long enough to be acquired if not to reach the promised land of being cash flow positive. Tell me who is going to make it all happen, not the advisory board or even the board of directors, but who is going to be working 15 hours a day, seven days a week in managing the affairs of the company. Tell me, in nontechnical terminology what the product or service is and why there is a need for it and how big that need should be.

Also important for you to accept is the fact that there is enormous competition for private company investment. In my role as a company consultant and investment banker, I am almost always in a position of seeking financing for several companies which I consider to be highly attractive opportunities for investment.

First and perhaps the most important point I will make, is that it makes all the difference in the world if the author or party submitting the plan is someone who has been introduced to me by either someone I know or someone I don't know but who is in a responsible position. It makes little difference who the introducer is if it is not someone I know well. They can be partners in a law firm, partners in an accounting firm, the vice president of the bank the entrepreneur has used for a while, the professor at a university who had the entrepreneur as a student, a prior employer, the patent attorney used by the entrepreneur, a successful business owner known to the entrepreneur or just someone who can and will vouch for the intelligence and integrity of the individual. Investing is a people assessment business and the seeker of funds should make it as easy as possible for the prospective provider of funds to learn about and eventually respect him or her.

Fiduciaries are, by law and moral convention, the guardians of other people's assets and as such are subject to greater criticism and liability if they lose money than they are rewarded if they are successful in protecting assets. The image of a professional investor in private companies being a fast draw cowboy, one who willingly takes chances on slim odds is simply wrong. The professional investor is a calculating, risk adverse, individual who usually wants or even needs to have the responsibility reduction of others investing with him. All too frequently a "yes" from a venture capitalist really means "we will do the deal if we or you can persuade other professional investors, of which we approve, to take between 20% and 80% of the deal." The justification for such a "we only want a small piece of specific deals" approach is one of both spreading the risk but also of having a wider range of investment managers caring about and being willing to assist, with contacts and advice, the recipient of the funds.

If most professional investors really do not want to lose money and that is their career focused objective then how can entrepreneurs bring them from the point of fear of loss to the point of departure where their natural greed will prompt the desired investment? Most entrepreneurs focus their fund-raising pitches on an assumption of greed versus fear on the part of the investor, just because the investor may proclaim their willingness to accept risk. It's a mistake. The reason people fear the dark is because the dark represents the unknown. Entrepreneurs seeking funding should focus on helping their prospects gain confidence in safety and therefore see the light and logic of investing.

Let's start backwards. What would the professional investor recriminate himself about if a loss occurs? Such statements as "I should have researched the people better," "I should have checked the competition for the product or service better," "I should have structured the deal where I had more control to make changes earlier in the process if projected events didn't occur" and "I should have known they were not asking for enough money or didn't have enough management experience to make it work." These are the sort of thing they might say about their losers and you can think of more. OK, now let's address how we would respond in the presentation of the opportunity and deal structure to these very natural and predictable reactions.

Managers: increasingly successful private company investors will only invest in companies where the CEO has a history of prior managerial success. They do not want to be tuition payers for good people to become good managers. They want someone who is already experienced in managing a company. Yes, of course, this requirement for experienced management would have kept many from having invested in Federal Express, Microsoft and other wonderful winners at early stages. The usual approach is for the entrepreneur to attempt to attract the participation of just such an experienced manager, usually giving the individual between 10% and 30% of the pre-money, promotional shares, and the promise of a competitive salary. The other attempt to address the need for experience is the creation of Advisory Boards as well as attracting experienced and visible business people as members of the Board of Directors.

Let's consider the areas of concern and fear regarding a relatively new enterprise on the part of a prospective capital provider—and also some possible answers. They include:

- **The product or service can't be produced with the funds predicted.** In the movie financing and construction businesses a completion bond is used to assuage the fear of non-completion. Is it possible the entrepreneur might obtain a third party guarantee of completion? Might the entrepreneur pledge all or a portion of his shares in the enterprise to the investor subject to completion, if appropriately defined? Can the benefits to the company and therefore the investor be quantified even if the product or service isn't completed satisfactorily? Surely there has to have been some benefit derived by the company from being in business for a given period even if the product or service being developed didn't pass muster. Was there a residual benefit of relationships, partial product development, new discoveries (even were they only relating to the other products which were in the market competing) and was there value in the team and collective talents which had been created? Just show me the exercise wasn't an all or nothing play and that I will have something left of value under a worst case scenario.

- **The product or service can't be sold as anticipated in terms of price or number of units.** Advance orders, even if non-binding and subject to quality, price and customer acceptance, are the most compelling evidence of customer acceptance of the idea of the product, even before the product is available. If advance orders cannot be obtained then can letters of prospective customer interest in being advised of the availability of the product or service when ready be obtained? Clearly, most entrepreneurs should be able to get a statement from a prospective customer that they would be willing to consider buying the product or service from the company if the company could satisfactorily produce the product or service and be willing to sell it at a price the customer found attractive. Far too many entrepreneurs assume successful marketing will just happen once they have the product or service ready for sale. That is not the way the world works. Everything has to be sold and, indeed, a lot of products are produced for which there isn't and never was sufficient market demand to warrant the product's creation. The intelligent investor wants to be assured the product can be sold at a price which will afford a satisfactory profit to the company being considered for investment.

- **The product cannot be financed, even if it can be produced and marketed.** One of the reasons for doing a business plan is to think through and present the issues of financing of sales. Of course, the financing of sales is a better problem to have than the running of a business not having any sales to finance. However, the experienced investor will want to be assured the company will be able to finance the inventory, work in process, delivery, etc.—and do so without having to pay unexpectedly high finance charges—if they are successful in getting orders. Letters from a bank or finance company setting forth their interest in participating and the general terms on which such assistance might be available are useful in planning the business and in demonstrating to investors how well the entrepreneur has thought through the development of the business.

- **There really isn't a significant market for the product or service.** Although advance orders or indications of interest are the best evidence of potential customer demand there are other means possible. An independent market research firm can survey the market in terms of future customer prospects. Such a firm can also survey present and potential competitors re their current product offerings. The report or findings of such a firm can be vital in planning and investment presentation.

- **Even if there are sales will the market permit the company to earn a good profit?** Note the phrase "good profit." There is no incentive to invest in companies which are not likely to produce superior profits. Will the product or service be of such customer benefit so as to allow a premium pricing? How easy will it be for competitors to offer comparable products or services? Is there really meaningful patent protection available and will the company be able to afford to obtain worldwide patents—and to defend them? The value of patents is one of permitting product pricing to be other than truly competitive.

- **Will the company be profitable even if the revenue projections are achieved and are the projections realistic?** Investment bankers, professional investors and accountants are probably the groups which spend the most time reviewing financial statements and projections. Therefore a letter from one or more such types affirming the reasonableness of the projections could go a long way toward helping a prospective investor get to a comfort zone. The more responsible people, using recognizable letterheads, who can offer support for elements of the business plan, the better for the entrepreneur.

- **Are the people listed in the business plan capable and honest?** Letters of reference are better than a listing of references for the key people. An investor should want assurance as to the competence and integrity of those in whom investment is being considered. Depending on the type of business insurance company fidelity bonding might be desirable or even required in certain businesses, such as investment brokerage.

Now let's address the issues of control of the company and if and when there should be a change in the control structure. The Board of Directors of a company control the company and has the ability to terminate and replace all officers of the company. Therefore, the numeric control of the Board of Directors is significant.

Although investors in private companies do not typically want to take an active management role in a company in which they are investing, they do, however, usually want an increasingly active role as they feel their investment is being threatened by projections not being achieved as predicted. Therefore the issue is addressed by agreeing to elect an increasing number of directors as predicted events do not occur. Similarly, the entrepreneur, usually the CEO at the time of initial capital seeking, can either provide a signed but undated resignation or agree to a change in function in the event something on which the investor was counting didn't occur.

Board representation is a two-edged sword entrepreneurs frequently misinterpret. The entrepreneur somehow usually feels it is an honor to serve on the board of a company and that in offering to elect directors a great gift is being bestowed. I believe that quite the contrary is the case. It is the director who is giving the company the benefit of his or her experience and advice as well as being willing to accept the risk of time and liability associated with the provision of service. In my books and talks intended to assist investors I advise the investors to require "Observation Rights" as a part of their investment agreement and also to have the right to appoint one or more directors, but not to become a member of the Board of Directors.

If the concern of the prospective investor is one of loss then consider creating packages of collateral which can be pledged to secure capital in the form of loans where on the failure of certain predicted events the collateral becomes the partial or complete property of the investor.

Also consider the possibility of granting stock or stock options to investors, increasing their possible profit in the company, in the event predicted events do not occur. Investors invest based upon predictions even though they know that most predictions are not likely to be achieved. Therefore if the predictions they feel they should be compensated for are not achieved they are entitled to a bonus as they are bearing additional risk over that expected.

Return on Investment—whose and how much? The ROI anticipated by the investor is a function of that which is received in some form as a result of having accepted a known level of risk. If the investor doubles the amount invested over five years then approximately a 15% annual average compound return has been earned. There are lots of tables showing the rates of return. In my case, I seek a minimum return of a 44% annual average compound return and typically structure deals to yield a 3-fold return in three years to achieve that result.

But what is the ROI from the perspective of the entrepreneur? Typically, the entrepreneur has not invested a great deal in the company, though it may be more than 100% of his or her net worth. Frequently, the entrepreneur accepts a compensation package, including fringe benefits and perks, which is less favorable than he or she could have earned working for someone else. I have often thought it would be useful to assign values to the elements of the entrepreneur's contribution so the investor could be better aware of the full investment being made in comparing ROI's.

The pre-money valuation of a company seeking investors is one of the negotiated points which is most difficult to address as frequently the entrepreneur does not have the breadth of knowledge necessary to know of a large number of truly comparable companies. Also the timing of the assessment is critical and when comparing publicly traded companies and private companies there are, and in some cases should be, large scale differentials. I try to avoid the issue by focusing on the investor's guaranteed, minimum, return based upon predicted events rather than guessing valuations. Some of the more amusing reading one can do is reading valuation reports regarding early stage, technology driven companies.

The investor will be justifiably concerned by the prospect of a sale or merger proposal recommended by management as if the investor does not go along with the recommendation then the management and the investor are likely to have future problems. All too frequently deals are made where the management fares significantly better than do the investors through the operation of compensation and stock option packages in which the investors do not participate. Addressing the matter as a future possibility in the investment agreement can lessen an investor's apprehension.

The last points I would make are perhaps the most important or, at least, different from those which other experts will discuss.

Investors are transients by definition. Investors buy into companies only in order to sell, at a future point in time. Entrepreneurs start companies for many reasons, but that is the subject of another talk and a few books, not including necessarily selling out. The company started by an entrepreneur is the entrepreneur's child and playpen. The company is a statement about and by the entrepreneur. The company can provide a lifestyle and power base satisfactory to the entrepreneur all without selling the company, not so for the investor. Therefore, the investor wants or should want, in most cases, an exit plan.

I handle these sometimes conflicting needs by requiring the company repurchase, at the option of the shareholder, the shares of the company sold to investors at an agreed price at an agreed time. The price can simply be a multiple of purchase cost or the price can be established as a function of the price earnings or other ratio's ratio of a previously agreed basket of comparable companies.

Conventional wisdom is that investors buy shares of a company and profit by the increasing value of the shares. Ultimately, it makes little difference, except as to the number of shares or percentage of shares held, whether the investor bought shares or convertible preferred stock, convertible debt or debt with warrants as if successful the company's stock will have an ascertainable value and if unsuccessful the company is unlikely to be able to meet its commitments.

But what about viewing capital as a fungible commodity an entrepreneur rents such as the renting of an office, equipment or even people—all things a company needs. Now what about paying rent on the basis of a percentage of sales—as the use of the money is critical to all of the other factors? I call the instrument providing for a percentage of sales rent (as is frequently used by landlords in shopping malls) or royalty (as is used in entertainment, publishing, extractive industries and with inventors), a "Revenue Participation Certificate" or RPC.

RPCs can be used in a range of ways. RPCs can be for a fixed percentage of sales, for sales only in excess of a given level, they can increase or decrease as sales increase, they can have a minimum and they can be capped, they can be secured or third party guaranteed, they can be negotiable and transferrable, they can be for fixed periods or for an event triggered period of time. RPCs can be paid regardless of a company's profits or only subject to profits. Also RPCs can be convertible into equity, at either party's option, depending on the terms of the agreement. RPCs result in income for the recipient and an expense for the company. RPCs allow entrepreneurs to retain equity and investors to be less concerned with the manner in which companies are managed.

I most often use RPCs as the fee or inducement to issue bank loan guarantees but they can be also be used to obtain credit in other forms. RPCs allow a capital provider to focus on the revenue line and likely trend of revenues without being as much concerned with the profitability or maximized efficiency of management.

Specifically as relating to investing in Less Developed Countries (LDCs), American professional investors are concerned by the lack of methods of dispute resolution which are available to them. They need to know that contracts, once negotiated and executed, can be enforced by courts and that judgments can be perfected. Absent such comfort the professional investor will want a much higher return from an investment made in an area without protection he considers normal than where contracts are readily enforceable.

In thinking about the challenge facing LDC entrepreneurs in obtaining U.S. and European investment capital I have reached a conclusion the LDC entity should attempt to affiliate, possibly as a joint venture partner, with an American or European firm and the affiliate entity, incorporated in a jurisdiction which is familiar to the professional investors being solicited, should then be the entity approaching professional investors. The joint venture can transfer funds to the LDC party through license agreements, loans or some other methodology. The logical joint venture partner is a company already engaged in a similar business or research area. The engagement can be as a supplier, a customer or even a possible competitor.

The proposition put forth by the joint venture would be something like, "we are in the same field or are knowledgeable about the field, we are known and checkable entities here in a jurisdiction which is comfortable for the professional investor and we are prepared to devote the energy to have continuing collaboration with the LDC group." It's an appealing pitch, combining the assets of the occidental partner with the resources of the Asian or other LDC partner for the benefit of all concerned."

Entrepreneurs need capital to translate visions to realities and professional investors need entrepreneurs to create value and enhance the capital for which they are responsible. Both parties have specific needs and the art of the game is to find a means of accommodating the needs of the parties—and I hope some of these thoughts have helped.

Fair question—for angels to ask entrepreneurs

In the process of attempting to acquire funds with which to create and develop a business entrepreneurs make many statements to those they seek to attract as capital providers. Following are some questions which the Angel might ask as prompts for constructive dialogue.

- What will happen to the company if the revenues and earnings projected on a worst case basis are not achieved as predicted?
- When will the company run out of money in the event the development of the enterprise is at a slower rate than expected?
- If the company has to be liquidated or is forced to sell how much money, net of that you have received as cash compensation, will you and others in management making the projections on which the investors based their judgment and lost have invested?
- Which companies or individuals are most likely to want to buy whatever is left of the company if it is unsuccessful?
- What might be the first indication the company will not be able to achieve its goals and objectives?

- When and under what conditions should the CEO and management of the company be changed?

- How has the fairness of the valuation of the funds being sought been derived or justified?
- Who else has been approached to provide funds for the project?
- What will the proposed managers of the enterprise do if the project does not proceed?
- What has been the experience of the managers in terms of enriching investors in their previous activities?
- Will the managers of the enterprise invest cash in the business on the same terms and conditions as is being sought from investors?
- Would the managers of the business making the projections invest funds, if loaned to them by the investor or others, in the enterprise on the same terms and conditions as is being proposed to the investor?
- What is the proportionate profit potential relative to cash investment between the investor(s) and the managers in the event the business is as successful as predicted?
- What is the single most important event predicted about the enterprise and what will happen if it does not occur when anticipated?

As most human endeavors fail to achieve the results originally hoped for the above questions are fair and reasonable as the Angel investor is being asked to accept the predictions made by those seeking to entice the Angel and capture his capital.

The future for venture capital investing organizations

As presented to the Global Software Seminar
sponsored by the University of Oulu, Finland
May 17, 2001

Recently I was asked my opinion as to the future for venture capitalists (VCs), especially in light of the changes in investee company valuations occurring during the past 12 months.

The bottom line is that I believe it is predictable the model which VCs will morph into will be that of traditional European merchant banks.

The principals of organizations having capital to invest almost always believe they have superior business decision making abilities than those company managements in which they have invested. Having the power to employ capital produces an arrogance as well as both a need to make judgments as to further supporting investee companies and a tendency to be highly and continually judgmental. This is especially true during periods of specific investee company or general economic stress.

Investors, continually having alternative investment opportunities to consider as well as being directly involved with other professional investors the capital providers, frequently as fiduciaries, tend to have greater sophistication than the management of the companies to which they have entrusted capital. They also frequently have an ability to access informational resources not available to the companies in which they have invested.

As there is a tendency for proactive VCs to become increasingly involved with the decision making of their investee companies, as evidenced by the increasing demand for board of director participation, the line between investor and manager tends to blur. Indeed, I advise investors not to become members of management through board representation but rather to require observation rights. Nevertheless, most VCs want to be on the boards of directors of the companies in which they invest.

For a range of reasons, most VCs currently prefer to provide capital using convertible preferred stock as the means of investment. There is, in the minds of some, a distinction between lending money to a company and investing money in a company in early stage enterprises. I believe the form of investment should be that which best suits the needs of the investor and that may be the same, but does not have to be, as that which the investee wants.

The needs of VCs as investors in privately owned companies is shaped by the form of their own capital as well as an overriding assumption that in the case of successful companies the companies will either be sold to a larger enterprise, for cash and/or stock, or partially sold to the public in an underwritten offering. The partnership capital structure used by most VCs is such that at the end of a specified number of years there is a dissolution and the assets distributed, less management fees. Therefore all decisions must recognize the end game and be made accordingly.

If VCs both have, and are able to persuade investors that they have, good business decision making skills and a continuing exposure to potentially profitable investment opportunities then I believe the capital structure of the industry is likely to change as VCs become increasingly proactive and involved with "their" companies.

I believe the corporate or possibly trust form of investment will replace the partnership form and that capital will be become permanent rather than transient. Of course, there are income tax considerations but these can be managed in the structuring of the new Venture Investing Companies (VICs).

The managers of the VICs, many of which will come to own most of the stock of their investee companies, can be rewarded by profit sharing payments in either or both the investee companies or the VIC itself.

The VIC could, as is already the case in some VCs and even in publicly traded holding companies, provide administrative and other services in return for fees.

The VIC could sell off all or a portion of their investee companies as well as reward management of the companies with profit shares and even equity.

The VIC would simply be a recognition of that which is naturally evolving. Liquidity, if necessary for capital marketing purposes, could be provided by the VIC agreeing to periodic repurchases of shares on the basis of either market value, were the VIC to be publicly traded, or some agreed measure of capital valuation.

Small Business Investment Companies and Business Development Companies, none of which have grown to the size and success of many within the venture capital industry, do have many of the features I believe will evolve for the VCs of the future. Perhaps it's a matter of tax treatment, high tech focus, physical location or capital marketing, but whatever it is the bulk of money for investing in early stage companies has gone to the VC community.

In conclusion, the future professional venture investor is likely to be more involved in fewer companies and have permanent capital to use. Also many, if not most, will be publicly traded—though, of course, they will not want to be governed by the strictures of the present SEC Investment Act(s).

What I've learned from the mistakes I've made about investing in private companies

I've learned a great deal during the past almost 50years regarding what to do and, more importantly what not to do, within the private company investment process—if earning an extraordinary risk related return is the investor's primary objective. Although I frequently make the same mistakes over again I also have an ability to find and make new mistakes to add to the list. The title of this talk suggested to my wife and some of my other friends that the length of the presentation could well be much longer than intended by those who honored me by arranging for my appearance here today and you would clearly have stopped listening before I stopped talking. Also a fuller cataloging of the mistakes made would (1) deter most of you from ever investing in a private company, which is not my intention and (2) lessen my inventory of horrors which I use when charging client companies a consulting fee.

Investing in private companies is enormously important for the country as a whole and for every community therein. Private company investment is an activity which should be favored, rather than penalized, by all governments in terms of tax relief and other legislation. Unfortunately it isn't. Elected politicians seem to yield more frequently to the voice of the electorate which, by definition, has neither the asset base permitting investment nor the entrepreneurial mind-set of employers, who are in a position, if financed, to make a positive difference to others.

In part, this is due to the lack of tangible recognition on the part of government as to the importance of fostering entrepreneurial activity which requires private company investors to demand a higher level of return from the entrepreneur than would otherwise be the case. It is almost as if the government is saying "we won't help you profit, even recognizing the risk which is being undertaken, and even though in success we, the government, win both directly in taxes paid, and only a bit less directly in the employment and general business activity created by the development of a successful enterprise." I believe we'd have a better functioning government if it were required that at least one-third of all elected representatives have been business founding employers (law firms being excluded) otherwise known as entrepreneurs. Incidentally, the exclusion of law firms is not on, as you might suspect, grounds of morality. Rather it is due to my perception of the result of the professional training of attorneys, which is to seek comfort only in finding precedent, rather than being the more right-brain dominant, innovative problem solvers, required to off-set those bureaucrats who are intellectually and emotionally captives of the past and fearful of change.

Mistakes made and lesson learned

Not understanding my own motivation—for being involved in a relationship without really knowing why. Why was I considering making an investment in a private company, any private company? Was it because I use a smiling face inside of the "(" as the "o" when I type the word "☺pportunity"? Was it because I am an incurable ☺pportunity and excitement junkie (as my wife would assert)? Probably so. Could it be because I really wished to help whoever was pitching me the ☺pportunity? Possibly so. In any case, whatever my motivation I damn well should understand what is driving me to become involved, as it is difficult for all and impossible for me to passively invest in private companies and therefore the investment should be expected to be more than just money. This is, of course, especially true as the recapture of the funds invested is usually dependent on the business succeeding. In the book *Venture's Financing and Investing In Private Companies* I list some of the reasons why people invest in private companies, other than to make a high return. It is surprising to me how few angels, those who spread their wings and open their wallets to entrepreneurs, are really only profit driven. Most have other than only profit on their agendas. Angels are frequently quite wonderful and interesting people and must be protected as were they to become extinct, due to more frequently than not, being the recipients of capital punishment, their losses become our losses, if their losses prompt them to abandon the exercise and leave the game.

Non-defining of success in considering an investment—For any of us to succeed we have to define success and to define success we have to have a clear vision of that which we are trying to achieve.

Do we crave power or a feeling of power and/or do we have a hope for recognition? Do we want to be a father-figure for an entrepreneur or his employees? Do we want to have an activity into which we can throw ourselves? Do we want to be in a position of the entrepreneur and others becoming dependent upon us? What do we want and how much of this want is responsible for our being willing to lose money?

I don't wish to suggest what anyone's motivation should be. I have just learned that we all would do a better job of investing to achieve an objective if we understood precisely the objective we were trying to achieve.

Not treating my money as if it weren't my money—Lots of times I have made the mistake of forgetting or failing to articulate what my objective was and have just gotten swept up in the challenge of making the deal—rather than continuing the decision making process, up until the time of closing, if I should do the deal. That's when I've been investing my own money. I have not made the same mistake when I have been acting as a fiduciary. Therefore I urge all investors to pretend they are responsible for acting on behalf of others when making investments, especially in private companies. I promise you that a much better quality decision will be made if you think of yourself as a fiduciary.

Fear—and allowing my fears to unreasonably determine the deals that I will and won't do and how they are structured. What am I most fearful of in making investments in private companies? Losing the money invested? No. I am prepared to lose that which I invest and I recognize that losing all of the money invested in any single private company, especially those which have the greatest early stage potential, is a reasonable possibility. That which frightens me most is that I may become liable for more than has been invested by virtue of investing more money in the deal to save or protect the money originally invested and probably more accurately "already lost." I describe such follow-on investments as "investment hostage" or ransom payment investing, being the practice of investing new money to recapture or resuscitate already lost, dead, capital. I have seen but a very few instances where follow-on investments, prompted by disappointing results, have yielded a satisfactory result or return. Usually they just increase the ultimate loss of the investor. I am also concerned with the possibility of becoming so involved in trying to assist the company in which I've invested that I end-up putting myself in a position where it can be asserted that I have incurred personal liability. For instance, no one wants to have a director's liability in a company having or causing environmental problems or employee and/or customer harm.

Fear of loss in investing is probably a good thing to have as long as the fear is not at such a level as to immobilize the investor. A key lesson taught and learned at Paris Island and later in Korea was "move, don't freeze, when receiving fire." Investing successfully in private companies has some of the same elements as combat and the investor has to be prepared to be in motion, and not just stay in a fox hole of inactivity, waiting for it all to pass or for the "one he never hears." I've learned not to be afraid to take affirmative action to protect the invested assets for which I am responsible.

In structuring transactions I've learned to first determine my investor candidate's priorities. If I am structuring an investment ☺pportunity for truly affluent investors, not just those purportedly qualifying as "accredited," I focus on risk analysis and abatement as rich people do not want to be embarrassed by losses as they recognize they have no monetary motivation to expose themselves to risk. If I am attempting to appeal to a broader range of investors then I focus more on the possible magnitude of gain and favorable risk/reward relationship. After all greed is but a fear of not profiting to a maximum level, much as being obsessed with physical fitness reflects a fear of being sick and frail.

Being greedy—resulting in my embracing the entrepreneur's vision of success and future profits. We all want to win, however we define the win and, as I've noted previously, it is vital that we do define for ourselves the definition of the win.

Why have I accepted sales and earnings projections which require the acceptance of the entrepreneur's product or service without the company having made the level of marketing investment similar to that of other comparable and competitive companies? Why have I not required the entrepreneur to respond to a series of "what if" questions such as what if you die or become an alcoholic, are faced with a patent infringement action, lose your key engineers or salespeople, the primary vendors on whom you are depending for components go out of business, the primary sales prospect decides not to buy, the bank doesn't do that which you expect them to do and finally, it takes twice as long to develop the product and/or make the sales envisioned? Why? Because I wanted to make the investment, gain a participation in the project and get rich as a result.

Being lazy—too lazy to thoroughly check the background of the entrepreneur, even though I had the ☺pportunity to do so. Few of us really enjoy the process of prying into the lives of others. However, as once money has been committed to private company investment it become a captive of the process. Therefore, it is vital that we really know who it is we are, all too frequently, "giving" our money to. Many of us know what to do and simply fail to do it when it comes to researching an investment ☺pportunity.

Being cheap—as in being unwilling to recognize that making investment decisions requires the expenditure of funds. A professional background check on an entrepreneur will cost in the area of $1,500 if more than a litigation and credit check is involved. It is money well spent.

In one case recently an associate of mine and myself paid $7,500 for the preparation and distribution of a newspaper insert marketing effort on behalf of a company whose product interested us. Copies of the insert for San Diego Photo Restoration Services are in the room. If the insert drew as few as 150 responses in a 22,500 business journal distribution then we'd get our $7,500 back and know that we would make money by rolling out the service nationally. If we didn't recapture the marketing money then we'd have learned something which would save us a lot more than the $7,500. By the time I present this talk we will have known if we made or saved money.

In another case, I recently advised and arranged for a client to have a background check run on a charismatic individual who had proposed a joint venture. The background of the individual it was learned included several jail terms and lots of litigation. Needless to say, the relationship did not occur as had been originally contemplated, though there may be a different form and level of relationship.

In some cases, professional investors seek to recapture from a funding (and sometimes even without a funding occurring) their legitimate due diligence expenses through the imposition of an investigation fee or reimbursement agreement. My approach has been to require the entrepreneur to pay the entire cost of our due diligence if we uncover significant factual data which is in opposition to that which the entrepreneur presented to us or which is relevant and negative and should have been disclosed. It is going to cost, one way or another, at least $5,000 to $10,000 to professionally reach a decision of whether or not to invest in a private company assuming the proposition is not rejected out of hand. Private company investors must either be willing to spend the money or trust to their intuition, experience-based judgment and/or luck. Again, were you investing as a fiduciary you'd probably spend the money—and obtain a better overall portfolio result.

One of my friends who is an active and experienced smaller enterprise consultant, who assists companies in organizing themselves, prepare a business plan and obtain financing, reminds me that one of the aspects of both being cheap and of denying the ever present efficacy of Murphy's Law is being under insured. Also too few entrepreneurs are pressed by those investing in them to set aside, beyond their control, amounts sufficient to assure the expense of remaining in "good legal standing" for subsequent years after the investment is made. If the company fails to maintain its legal standing then it can loose its right to litigate or even effectively contract. Strange and murky things happen when companies get into trouble and some of them can be guarded against by experienced investors overriding the entrepreneurs super abundance of confidence that all will be well because that's the way it has to be (in his eyes).

Becoming dependent—upon the entrepreneur as an individual. Investing in private companies is a people assessment exercise as much as a financial analysis. I and most other private company investors usually know within a very short period of time, minutes or perhaps even seconds, if the entrepreneur is a person with whom a business relationship is wanted. However, I have paid the price of losing money by not requiring that there be more than one individual worthy of my admiration in a company being financed. Aside from the fact that entrepreneurs, though many would dispute the fact, are mortal, there should be in place a team of credible people on whom the investor can rely. If the entrepreneur being financed only attracts and recruits people of lesser quality and ability than he or she then there is a problem. Successful entrepreneurs frequently say the secret to their success was in hiring or attracting people who were smarter and better qualified than themselves. One of the distinctions between those having an entrepreneurial mind-set and those who think of themselves as inventors is that of the inventor being typically reluctant to share in the development of the intellectual property whereas the entrepreneur wishes to capture the resources and efforts of as many people as possible for his benefit.

Being non-diversified—in the creation and management of a portfolio of private company investments. None of us are so smart and experienced as to be able to predict which of the truly promising ☺pportunities we are exposed to, and with which we become involved, will be winners. We know that most will fail to achieve the initial objectives of the entrepreneur and some will actually fail. Therefore we should put ourselves in a position of "sprinkling money amongst talent" rather than restricting our investment to one or two private company investments, if we wish to be serious in the effort of making money. However, I and, I hope, you recognize that, again—it all goes back to the investor's motivation.

Being unrealistic—as to the absence of competition for the product or service being financed. Entrepreneurs all too frequently are either uninformed as to competitive factors or so very sure of themselves and secure in their vision that they minimize or discount the threat of competition. The result of such disregard of margin shrinking or revenue reducing competition is typically one of underestimation of the amount of funding required. Entrepreneurs typically under-estimate both the amount of time, and therefore money, required in reaching a point of being cash flow positive.

Being too tough—in the structuring of transactions. The essence of structuring a transaction is the shifting disproportionate amounts of reward to the stronger party and risk to the weaker party. The reality is that the stronger party, the one with the resource needed by the entrepreneur, has to be fair and make certain the entrepreneur understands why the deal is fair. In cases where the entrepreneur perceives that he is being taken advantage of a destructive and investment threatening attitude can develop. The investor should protect himself on the downside and be prepared to be generous with the entrepreneur on the upside. For this reason I prefer to provide risk capital in forms other than equity.

Falling in love—with an investment. Frequently there are ☺pportunities for the investor to recapture his investment while still retaining an interest in the enterprise. In most cases when I have had such ☺pportunities my greed and need for vindication of initial judgment has prevented my taking advantage of the ☺pportunity. Structuring transactions with an exit strategy is important and the difference between a professionally negotiated deal and one made by and with amateurs is the presence or absence of an exit. A frank and open discussion with the entrepreneur, prior to the making of the investment, is desirable in order that the entrepreneur understand the investor's need to recapture and recirculate capital. The investor in private companies should not confuse his role with that of the entrepreneur. We all have to know who we are in any given situation.

I hope the foregoing, perhaps all too revealing, disclosure of some of the mistakes I've made will allow you to avoid making the same mistakes. As noted at the beginning of this talk, I seem to have a wonderful ability of not only making some of the mistakes repetitively but of also finding new mistakes to make in investing in private companies.

Investing in private companies, when they become successful, is about as rewarding and satisfying an experience as one can have when dealing with money matters.   I urge those of you who can now or will be able to do so in the future to sprinkle money amongst talent by investing in a range of private companies, especially those, which if successful, have the scope to make all involved wealthy. It doesn't pay to invest in private companies having limited horizons such as single restaurants or retail establishments whereas investing in retail businesses having the potential of franchising could be an excellent idea.

Thank you for allowing me to share with you some of the lessons I've learned. I hope they memory of them may be of benefit to you at the point you are considering embarking on your private company investing adventure.

Part Two
GUIDE TO VENTURE FUNDING

THE LARRY & BARRY GUIDE TO Venture Funding

An illustrated manual for young entrepreneurs that will amuse and interest both the experienced entrepreneurs and entrepreneurial investors

Arthur Lipper III

With drawings by Robert Neubecker

Registered purchasers of this guide (registration card enclosed herein) will be entered without additional charge or payment of any kind in Venture's annual $1.0 million Entrepreneur of the Year Award lottery. The prize: $1.0 million paid at the rate of $1.00 per year for a million years, will be awarded to the entrepreneur who is able to raise the greatest amount through the sale of shares in the Award. The winner will be notified by an IRS agent.

This material has not been approved by any authoritative body or entrepreneurs, academics, venture capitalists or investors in private companies. Any statement to the contrary is false and will result in the guilty party being required to read a significant number of business plans.

Introduction

In Venture's monthly Chairman's Comment there usually appear our characterizations of an entrepreneurial team we call Larry and Barry. I use their nicknames, rather than their full names, Lawrence Lion and Bernard Beaver, because I feel so close to them and understand their situation so very well, having been there so many times myself.

Larry has a flair for marketing and is both persuasive and courageous. Barry is the hardworking chief operating officer and inside partner. Larry deals with the customers and Barry with the suppliers and creditors. Larry negotiates the amount of the credit lines and Barry has to deal with the repayments and minor details such as maturities, collateral and interest rates. Through the medium of Larry and Barry I try both to inform and amuse. Admittedly, it is easier to amuse those who recognize themselves in the situations being portrayed than those who haven't yet experienced these initiations into entrepreneurship.

In this Guide I also attempt to show some of the stages in the evolution of a venture's funding from the perspectives of both the entrepreneur and the investor. There is so much for young entrepreneurs to learn and so many times they find it necessary to reinvest the process. My hope is that this Guide will provide some insights to assist those on whom so many will depend for employment and inspiration.

The idea for *The Larry and Barry Guide to Venture Funding* occurred to me on a Saturday morning at 5:15 while my wife and I were watching a television news program. (Entrepreneurs are usually morning people.) By 8:30 I had done the rough sketches and captions. By 9:30 Barrie Stern, *Venture's* art and picture editor, had reached Bob Neubecker, the talented artist who translates my very rough sketches and ideas into our disarming characters. By mid-morning Rolando Mestre, *Venture's* director of production, was collecting data regarding paper and press availability and, of course, price. Jim Rogers, our national sales manager and Shawne Burke, circulation manager, were involved and focusing on their roles in the project. By Sunday morning I collected from Bob the first sketches and Barrie (even though she was on vacation) and I met to discuss them. By Tuesday Eileer Broderick, my harassed secretary, had all of the text typed and I made the original paste-up. Somewhere along the line I assigned the business aspects of the project to Ken Sgro, *Venture's* business manager. Monday night, at our typesetter's office, Jeannie Mandelker, our managing editor, and I discussed the project and by Tuesday afternoon it was almost complete, including a possible sale of advertising pages to a sponsor. Only with an intelligent and highly motivated staff could such an effort be successful. I am particularly fortunate to have such a team at *Venture* and thank all who helped. It's fun to be an entrepreneur when riding a wave.

Arthur Lipper III

Larry: *"I've had it. This company just doesn't understand anything other than memos, report forms, meetings, and seniority-based advancement. Their idea of a promotion is paying someone more to receive more memos, fill out more report forms, attend more meetings, and be responsible for more people whose horizons are limited."*

Barry: *"Right on. There must be a better way. If they can make a profit doing it so badly why couldn't we be successful doing it better? I've been thinking..."*

S uccessful entrepreneurs were usually successful, but frustrated, employees prior to going into their own business. They are usually goal- and achievement-oriented. Contrary to popular opinion, money is not the primary motivation for most entrepreneurs, except insofar as it signifies success and gives them more mobility. Getting something accomplished better or differently is the usual objective.

Barry: *"With a little luck, if we had enough money and could get the right people, at the right price, and if market factors remained constant, we could be profitable by the fourth year and make some real money in the fifth year."*

Larry: *"And that's being very conservative. Look what happens to these numbers if we just assume a 25% increase in sales in the last three years."*

Projecting revenues and profits is both the most difficult and important job for any entrepreneur starting out in business. It usually takes significantly longer to develop revenues, and therefore positive cash flow, let alone profits, than anticipated. The projections must be sufficiently attractive to both the entrepreneur and investor to justify their investment of resources. Almost all new business plans assume losses in the first two years, a break-even in the third year, and increasing profits thereafter. The difficulty of making projections is frequently compounded by the entrepreneur's own inexperience and the fast moving nature of the industry. The entrepreneur is also faced with the reality that investors can currently, without risk or effort, earn high rates of return and that the opportunity he represents must afford a significantly hither, seemingly assured, return to be risk/reward competitive. Frequently, worst case projections are so conservative that they do not provide sufficient incentive to take on the investment risk.

Larry: *"Now we just have to mail these business plans and the personalized letters to the venture capitalists you found on Venture's list."*

Barry: *"I'm sure glad you thought of stamping each of them 'confidential.' That'll show them this is important stuff and that we trust them. They are being given a real ground-floor opportunity. But what are we going to do if they all say yes? It wouldn't be fair to do it on a first-come, first-served basis as some may be away from their offices and not able to respond for a week or so."*

Since venture capitalists receive thousands of unsolicited business plans, it's not certain that your plan will even be read, much less acted upon. My most helpful suggestion for getting around this is to try to have someone who knows the potential investor call or write to alert him to expect the plan. If you don't have a contact, an attorney, investment banker or senior executive of a successful company will at least be able to help in getting the plan read sooner than might otherwise be the case. The best reference would be an entrepreneur in whom the investor had already successfully invested. The more familiar the investor is with the contact, the better.

Such endorsements can be of great assistance to the entrepreneur. To be effective, the entrepreneur must meet the prospective investor or representative as early in the process as possible. The initial purpose of submitting the business plan is to capture the attention of the venture capitalist and interest him in investing his time to study the opportunity and subsequently to meet the entrepreneur. An early meeting is crucial and should be the focus of the entrepreneur's efforts. No positive decision is ever reached without a number of meetings. Therefore, the objective of the entrepreneur must be to get that meeting.

Remember, it is not possible for venture capitalists to study more than a small number of the plans received and it is even more difficult for them to meet with all of the entrepreneurs who prepare them. Introductions and endorsements are the name of the game. Never end an initial meeting without getting the name of at least one additional person who might be an investor candidate. If possible, obtain permission to use the name of the person making the suggestion in approaching the new prospective investor. Of course, if an introductory call can be made, that is even more helpful.

Larry: *"It's like there is both a mail and phone strike. I can't believe we're not getting responses, let alone offers. It's been more than a week since they must have received our plan. I've even checked to see if our address and phone number on the new stationery and plan are correct."*

Barry: *"Maybe those venture capitalists aren't as smart as we've read. They probably don't even understand the brilliance of our approach or that our skills are such that making the projections will be a snap."*

Entrepreneurs whose plans are clearly without interest to venture capitalists usually receive a "thanks, but no thanks" rejection more quickly than those whose plans may hold some interest. All entrepreneurs believe they have the skills necessary to accomplish the goals set out in their business plans and almost all believe their plans represent a clear opportunity for investor profit. Many entrepreneurs are brilliant, but few business plans are.

Entrepreneurs submitting plans should confirm the receipt of their plans by venture capitalists and ask the venture capitalist when, in their normal flow of review, an indication of interest might be expected. More important, the entrepreneur should use every opportunity to try to make an appointment to meet the venture capital firm's initial review person.

Larry: *"You tell him about how conservative our projections are and how we really believe we can make much more and in a shorter time. Also tell him why we are well equipped to do it better."*

Barry: *"And you tell him about how the customers love us and will purchase our product and how we are going to go public next year, or at the very latest the year after, as soon as we turn profitable. Also, he has to understand that he will triple his money in three years, or perhaps a little longer and we are letting them in on a real winner.*

Entrepreneurs must demonstrate a high level of self-confidence to convince professional investors to fund their ventures. But the entrepreneurs also must realize that they are hardly objective about their own proposals. Most people who make projections believe them to be conservative or at least attainable.

Also, the entrepreneur must understand that professional investors can currently double their money in less than six years, while taking little risk and expending little effort, through the purchase of discount obligations of creditworthy debt issuers. Therefore, the prospect (remote) of tripling in three years is not exceptionally attractive when there is present certain substantial risk and probable effort. The assurance to the investor of an initial public offering also displays a lack of sophistication regarding both the securities markets and the probability of becoming profitable within a two-year period.

Barry: *"Damn, she was tough. Who'd 've thought she'd been involved in all those deals? She asked hard questions and really seemed to know our business."*

Larry: *"And at first when she asked if we wanted coffee I though she was a secretary. How'd she get so smart so young? Maybe she's right and we should redo the business plan and include a 'competitive section' and a changing interest rate scenario."*

There are a number of good venture capital investors who happen to be women and entrepreneurs should not make assumptions about who is going to review their plans.

Investors will be favorably impressed by the entrepreneur who has done his homework. Entrepreneurs should investigate the prospective investor and know something about the company's policies and personnel. The information is available from Venture Magazine, other directories, press clippings, and various advisory services.

Also, entrepreneurs can derive great benefit from the free critiquing of a business plan that is a part of the investment review and interview process. The business plan is, or should be, a living document which is constantly updated and improved. This is just one of the reasons why the broad, shotgun approach of sending out scores of business plans is a wasteful exercise. By sequential prospecting, the business plan submitted each time should be better and include more of what the entrepreneur has learned. Each rejection can be positive if something is learned.

Larry: *"He's the eighth vulture capitalist to say the same thing."*
Barry: *"How can they all be so stupid?"*

True, there is frequently a shared view on the part of professional investors. This is more likely because they have learned from similar previous experience than as a result of intellectual deficiency. The entrepreneur should try to learn why the venture capitalist has reacted as he has. It's just possible the venture capitalist is not the stupid one in the equation. If eight have turned a project down for similar reasons there is probably little benefit in pursuing it with similar organizations. The entrepreneur should either change the business idea reflected in the plan, its presentation, or the type of investor being contacted.

Larry: *"We've redone the damn plan now four times, included all of their ideas, and still can't get them to invest in us. They won't even negotiate with us. Remember when we thought that'd be the hardest part and were willing to be beaten down to a 50/50 deal?"*

Barry: *"How can all of these junkie companies go public showing losses or only tiny earnings? We're really sitting here on a gold mine and can't get any of those dumb investors to trust us with a little of their money."*

Entrepreneurs who have been rejected frequently develop a dislike for investors and come to think of them as either dumb or greedy. This is an attitude that is inevitably destructive when conveyed to the investors and makes an investment less likely. Successful entrepreneurs, those who gain custody of other people's money, understand the legitimate concerns and needs of the investor.

It does entrepreneurs little good to compare their projects to lower quality deals that are being sold to unsophisticated public investors through underwriters whose interests are not always consistent with those of the investors. The entrepreneur should compare this opportunity with companies which the investor can see as successful models for the entrepreneur's situation. Contrasting your company to junk cheapens it.

However, entrepreneurs should study and know all about the companies with which they hope to compete. They should analyze the operating ratios, financial statements, brokers, lawyers, auditors, and advisors to the competition. A sure knowledge of the competition is necessary to compete and also to make business plan projections which reflect the competitor's strategy.

If the entrepreneur thinks he's been rejected because the investor doubts his ability in some area he should ask the investor what specifically is wrong and attack the problem. If it is his youth or inexperience that is the problem, he should affiliate with someone who will provide the missing confidence factor. Similarly, if the investor is worried because he thinks the entrepreneur lacks some specific skill or training, other individuals can be added to the management team to close the gap. If the entrepreneur learns of the investor's true objections he can then manage them.

Larry: *"You indicate that you have helped lots of successful companies by offering both advisor and money-raising services. Can you help us and will you take stock in our company?"*

Barry: *"How is it that someone as successful as yourself doesn't need more of an office and a full-time staff?" We know that you believe in keeping 'lean and mean' and that you do most of your work in client offices but don't you find these quarters a little inconvenient?*

"Also, do you think we might negotiate something more modest than your normal minimum fee of $2,000 a day, plus reimbursement of unlimited and non-accountable expenses, plus an additional 'success' fee of 10% of the money we receive from people you recommend we approach? And how about the 10% of our stock you get that you say helps ensure your continuing interest in our company? Also, do we have to have the 12-month exclusive agreement with you?"

It's not unusual for entrepreneurs to be preyed upon by inept, though frequently persuasive management consultants. The rule for entrepreneurs is very simple. Ask the "consultant" or "investment banker" for a list of those for whom he has provided service, on the same terms as is being sought, within the last year or two. If there is a reluctance to disclose his clients then beware. The entrepreneur is very vulnerable and gets ripped off frequently by those promising service and/or funding. Entrepreneurs should, to the extent hey can, cultivate relationships with successful investors who have the respect of the financial community and whose prestige will, in turn, enhance the entrepreneur's reputation.

Larry: *"I'm sure glad you read that book on investing in private companies and got the idea about 'angels' who invest in private companies. This guy seems to have lots of money and can't be a dumb as the 53 venture capitalists who either turned us down or wouldn't even see us."*

Barry: *"And we only need five more of his friends and we can get started."*

Less than half of one percent of all new startup companies receive any investment from professional investors. Most new companies are financed by the entrepreneur himself and his family and friends. "Angels," those who invest in private companies not as professionals, and frequently not for conventional profit motives, are the entrepreneur's best probable external source of funding. The angel might well want to help the entrepreneur, or the community, or just have the fun of participating in the creation of a new venture. He usually has other affluent friends, as well as a range of business and banking relationships. The angel who has started his own business can be particularly helpful to a new company. Getting into the network of angels is a big step forward on the road to funding. Entrepreneurs who develop good relationships with successful angels, who are themselves entrepreneurs, are in a better position that those who get institutional financing because they have acquired an experienced partner as well as an investor.

Larry: *"He must have read that same damn book."*

Barry: *"But he did say that 'on his terms' he'd invest personally and help us find the rest. I liked the part where he said we could use his lawyer."*

Entrepreneurs will find that there are both angels and angel-sharks. The entrepreneur is not well advised to use the lawyer of the investor (though the investor is clearly better off if he does) as there will undoubtedly be instances of conflicting interests. It's inevitable that the relationship between investor and entrepreneur will at times be adversarial but this does not mean that it has to be ugly or destructive. It is just that the parties have differing objectives and perspectives. The offer of the angel to invest his money, not money of other, is significant.

The chances are that an experienced and intelligent angel will cut a fair deal with the entrepreneur because he realizes that the success of the business is in the hands of the entrepreneur and deals that work out the best are those that are fair to all concerned.

Larry: *"Some of those angel-investors are really sharp and have themselves actually started and managed a business. Our only problem is that if we don't make at least our worst case projections their halos will grow horns and their wings will be replaced with tails and pitchforks."*

Barry: *"Maybe they should be called 'convertible' angles. Well at least we're in business. We'll be making less salary, working harder and longer, and have to find solutions to problems we never knew existed. It should be fun and, with good fortune and good advice, there's no way we can fail."*

And Barry is right. The marriage has begun and if the parties have a mutual understanding and respect for each other's needs and strengths, it may work out. The entrepreneur, for example, can draw on the angel's experience for advice. Angels can give advice, or course, but have to be careful to allow the entrepreneur the independence he needs to make a success of the new business. If both sides are open about their needs success will be easier to achieve.

More of Larry and Barry

Our intrepid entrepreneurs, Larry and Barry, have been developing their business acumen in the pages of *Venture* since February 1984. Through their foibles we hope to help all entrepreneurs, both fledgling and those with vast experience, avoid some of the pitfalls on the road to success. We're reprinting some of our favorites for those of you who might have missed them, or forgotten what you learned, the first time around.

Larry: *"These, of course, are only our minimum projections."*

Projections, and the investor's natural wish to accept them, even when they seem improbable, are the basis for subsequent friction between entrepreneur and investor. Sounder deals would be made by investors if they understood the difficulty of predicting future events with accuracy. Similarly, entrepreneurs would have an improved relationship with investors if they could persuade them to invest without relying on predictions. One way to do this is by using the Lipper Equitable Distribution formula which is outlined in detail in Venture's Guide to Investing in Private Companies. According to this formula the investor initially owns all of the shares, and the entrepreneur has an option to buy shares from the company at the investor's per share costs plus interest. This tends to remove the necessity of persuading the investor of anything other than that the business prospects are good and the management competent. The shares optioned to the entrepreneur can be on terms that reflect the degree of progress achieved.

Barry: *"Now tell the professor about our scientific advisory board and the stock options."*

One important aspect of entrepreneurial management is the assembly of a team of people most qualified to achieve the desired objective. Entrepreneurs are more likely to recruit technical talent from academia than are other business executives. Academics are frequently content to leave their entire commercial interest in the hands of the entrepreneur because they are aware of the success of some academics who have done so, and want to have little contact with the for-profit community. Many investors associate academia with honesty simply because of the supposed lack of commercialism in the academic world. Thus, the entrepreneur can market the academics' presumed talent and integrity to investors.

Larry: *"They said they wanted a more orderly progression of earnings. So make the third year at least break even, and take some profit out of the fifth year."*

Barry: *"What did he mean by 'worst case?' Worst case is we don't get the money."*

Entrepreneurs react to the comments and requirements of the investors with whom they are in contact and frequently tailor their business plans to their wishes. The entrepreneur believes his own projections because, in many cases, he believes that he can do almost anything and can control his environment.

Larry: *"Our friends and customers will buy most of the shares offered."*

Underwriter: *"Of course, we want to be your financial consultants. Also, we want an exclusive representation agreement and right of first refusal to protect our clients."*

Barry: *"And with interest we earn on the new money, our earnings will be terrific."*

The negotiations surrounding a public offering reflect a combination of hope, naivete', cynicism, and institutionalized greed. Seldom do any of the participants want to cause the investor loss. All of the players, however, want the greatest gain for their own interests, short- and long-term. In most negotiations between underwriter and entrepreneur, the entrepreneur is at a disadvantage. The underwriter is usually more sophisticated and controls the process by which his firm will provide the funds the entrepreneur wants. Also, the underwriter can point out to the entrepreneur the positive results of an increase in the price of the shares which is frequently used to justify the fees, expenses, and warrants that the underwriter claims for himself at the outset.

Larry: *"I'm sure we're almost there."*

Barry: *"I think you're right. If we just keep on going straight we'll be fine."*

Entrepreneurs must be optimistic. Unfortunately they don't always see the possible problems which may interfere with their reaching their objectives.

There can be no doubt that entrepreneurs see things differently than non-entrepreneurs. They are much more right brain dominant than the general population, which means they are more creative and are better an conceptualizing than other people.

Barry: *"And even after we made our projections, they wouldn't wait."*

*"*Timing is everything" is a thought which is often best appreciated in retrospect. The entrepreneur must understand that there are macro developments that will dictate events affecting his business. Entrepreneurs must remain informed of events beyond the immediate environment.

If going public is a realistic and appropriate objective, then relationships with underwriters should be established before the underwriting. In other words, entrepreneurs should identify and initiate contact with the underwriter they'd most like in advance of generating the numbers to justify an underwriting. They should keep that underwriter apprised of progress. The underwriter then advises as to actions, and may even be willing to file an offering document earlier than would otherwise have been the case had there not been a continuing relationship and flow of information.

Larry: *"My wife has had it and she doesn't really believe we spend so much time here this late every night."*

Barry: *"My wife doesn't care anymore. The only reason she hasn't left me already is that she's afraid we might become successful."*

One of the problems that goes with the territory of being an entrepreneur, particularly a successful entrepreneur, is that of disproportionate focus on the business versus the family. Successful entrepreneurs, while in the process of building their business, tend to stay married longer than the general population. But they have a higher than normal divorce rate once the business becomes successful, is sold, or goes public. This is not to say that it is always the entrepreneur who initiates the separation. Frequently the spouse, in the face of the entrepreneur's success, also has an opportunity to cash in. The marriage partner may not have shared in the enjoyment of building the business. Investors in private companies are advised to find out about the marital situation of the entrepreneurs they finance because marital problems may affect the business.

Barry: *"The bank has finally called our loan."*

Larry: *"OK, so now our problem is also their problem and we have a new partner."*

The feared scenario of the entrepreneur unilaterally converting a creditor into a partner is such a real prospect that it frequently makes it difficult for the entrepreneur to obtain credit in the first place. No supplier of credit wants to find himself in the position of having to assist a borrower or customer purely for the purpose of obtaining the return of monies previously provided. It is one thing, as a provider of funds, to have an option to become an equity owner and an entirely different, and much less attractive, prospect of gaining control of a business as a creditor. Entrepreneurs should, at the time of difficulty, be already working closely with those supplying credit. The calling of a loan should neither come as a surprise to the borrower not occur without the lender having a full understanding of the ramifications. I created this representation, which is actually very much a cliché, with a great deal of reluctance as it so vividly displays the average lender's fears (prejudice) and assumption of the attitude of many entrepreneurs. It is my view that loans which must be called, rather than being amended to accommodate unforeseen events, are a result of either unintelligent borrowing or lending, and most frequently a combination of the two.

Larry: *"Remember when their vice president for acquisitions said we might have trouble adjusting to California if they decided to relocate our company?"*

Barry: *"Yes and remember when my wife said she would miss the different seasons too much to move?"*

The ultimate dream of many entrepreneurs is to either go public or sell their company to a larger company. Frequently going public is thought of as a means of accomplishing a sellout on better terms. This final, and admittedly somewhat fanciful, representation of entrepreneurial paradise is both insightful and slightly misleading. It is true that acquired companies are frequently relocated by the purchaser, at times as a means of making executive personnel changes and/or to bring the acquired company under closer control of the new parent. It is unlikely, however, that our friends Larry and Barry would abandon their entrepreneurial characteristics and become smugly satisfied with the newfound hedonistic environment...at least so I choose to believe.

Arthur Lipper III is the chairman and chief executive officer of *Venture, The Magazine for Entrepreneurs,* the fastest growing business magazine in America. Of the magazine's 300,000 subscribers, 144,900 "participated" in the formation of one or more new businesses in 1983 alone.

A venture capitalist and investment consultant, Mr. Lipper is also the author of *Venture's Guide to Investing in Private Companies* (Dow Jones-Irwin, 1984). He is the chairman of New York & Foreign Securities, Corp., a New York Stock Exchange member firm which specialized in serving financial institutions.

Mr. Lipper is the founder and chairman of the Association of Venture Founders, an organization for successful entrepreneurs. Although many of his recent projects are designed to stimulate entrepreneurship, he also has worked toward the identification and development of gifted children through both The Lipper Foundation and the Gifted Children Advocacy Association.

Through the medium of the Larry and Barry characters he created and who he believes embody the characteristics of many entrepreneurs, Mr. Lipper presents situations frequently experienced by those in the process of funding and managing businesses.

Published by *Venture Magazine, Inc.,* 521 Fifth Avenue, N.Y., N.Y. 10175